WHAT PEOPLE ARE SAYING ABOUT THE DIVINE CODE:

In The Divine Code of Da Vinci, Fibonacci, Einstein & YOU, Matthew Cross and Dr. Robert Friedman take one of Creation's great secrets and make it accessible, engaging and fun. This book offers you a cornucopia of delightful insights, enlivening practices and inspiring "A-ha's"!

Michael J. Gelb, bestselling author, *How to Think Like Leonardo Da Vinci* and *Da Vinci Decoded*

The Divine Code of Da Vinci, Fibonacci, Einstein & YOU is a profound accomplishment and contribution to the future of humanity. It is great that all this information is compiled in one place and provides the foundation and inspiration for us to apply the Divine Code. Thank you.

Debra Reynolds, founder of The Children's Dignity Project

The Divine Proportion is a scale of proportions which makes the bad difficult [to produce] and the good easy.

Albert Einstein

(The Golden Ratio is) The Secret of the Universe.

Pythagoras

...PHI (1.618) is the Most Beautiful Number in the Universe...

Dan Brown, *The Da Vinci Code*

I learned about the Golden Mean when I was about five years old... it greatly fascinated me.

Dr. Murray Gell-Mann, world-renowned physicist, Nobel Prize winner and author, ***The Quark and the Jaguar***

Nature's Path of Least Resistance and Maximum Performance follows the Golden Mean.

Dr. Ron Sandler, peak performance pioneer

The single most important biological structure, the DNA molecule, is in PHI (Golden Ratio) proportion.

Stephen Ian McIntosh, leading Integral theorist and author, ***Integral Consciousness and the Future of Evolution***

The great Golden Spiral seems to be Nature's way of building quantity, without sacrificing quality.

William Hoffer, author, *Midnight Express* and *Not Without My Daughter*

[The Golden Mean] is a reminder of the relatedness of the created world to the perfection of its source and of its potential future evolution.

Robert Lawlor, sacred geometer and author, ***Sacred Geometry: Philosophy and Practice***

The Fibonacci Sequence is a metaphor of the human quest for order and harmony among chaos.

Mario Merz, modern Italian Divine Code artist

THE
DIVINE CODE
GENIUS
ACTIVATION
Quote Book

MATTHEW CROSS &
ROBERT FRIEDMAN, M.D.

DISCLAIMER ~ NOTA BENE

The information and/or recommendations in this book are not meant to diagnose or treat any medical condition. Before beginning or following any of the nutritional recommendations, exercise protocols, training techniques, health improvement or any other health-related suggestions described in this book, please consult your physician or health care professional. The reader assumes 100% complete responsibility for any/all interpretations they may have and/or actions they may take and/or results they may enjoy as a result of reading this book. Neither the Publisher nor the Authors are liable for any loss, injury, damage or misunderstanding, which may occur from any interpretation and/or application of any of the information within this book.

The quotes featured within this book are from numerous sources, and are assumed to be accurate as quoted in their original and/or previously published formats. While every effort has been made to verify the accuracy of the featured quotes, neither the Publisher nor the Authors can guarantee or be responsible for their perfect accuracy. All websites, URLs and telephone numbers within this book were accurate at time of publication. However, websites may be modified or shut down and URLs or telephone numbers may change after publication without any notice. Therefore, the Publisher and Authors are not responsible in any way for the content contained in or missing/modified within any specific web site featured within this book.

The authors' insights and conclusions reached within this book are theirs alone, and—however provocative and mind-expanding they may be— may not be endorsed by any of the people, companies or organizations referenced within this book. The reader should know that this book is intended to be a holographic, gestalt approach to understanding and applying the principles outlined within it. Last yet not least, the authors are not responsible for any improvement, however small or great, in one's condition or for any sense of enlightenment or wonder that might result from reading, enjoying and applying the principles explored in this book.

Publishing Data
Published in the United States of America by Hoshin Media
PO Box 16791, Stamford, Connecticut 06905 USA

Made on a Mac. This book was written and designed on the incomparable computers made by the supremely talented people of Apple Inc.

Contents

The Quotes:

Φ

13 Remarkable Qualities of the Divine Code

1. **The Philosopher's Stone**—Your personal key to genius activation and universal wisdom.

2. **Universal Blueprint**—Guides the form and function of energy, matter, motion and life.

3. **Ubiquity**—Can be found virtually everywhere.

4. **Micro-Macro**—Manifests at all levels of reality, from the atomic to the galactic scale.

5. **Efficiency, Effortlessness and Flow**—Nature's Path of Least Resistance and Maximum Performance.

6. **Unifying**—Integrates parts into a greater, harmonious whole.

7. **Infinite**—Nature's premier irrational number, having no beginning and no end.

8. **Mysterious, Magical and Magnetic**—Has fascinated geniuses throughout history.

9. **Beauty, Harmony, Pleasure and Value**—Where the Code is found, so are these qualities.

10. **Timeless**—Appears as a powerful archetype in all civilizations.

11. **Evolutionary**—A path for continual growth, improvement and transformation.

12. **Open Secret**—Freely available to all at all times.

13. **Divine**—Spiritual tool for contemplating the infinite.

There is a code that lies both within and without. This secret yet open code points the way to your purpose, your happiness, your genius and your greatness... it goes by the name of The Divine Code.

Matthew Cross & Robert Friedman, M.D.

...the Golden Ratio has inspired thinkers of all disciplines like no other number in the history of mathematics.

Mario Livio, *The Golden Ratio: The Story of Phi, The World's Most Astonishing Number*

Φ

The Golden Section [Divine Code]... is a revelation fit to open the kind of fresh, incisive insight into the hidden heart of our universe that thrilled, and would again thrill, Pythagoras and Plato [and Da Vinci] and Copernicus and Kepler and Newton and Einstein. For it is part of the real music of the spheres, parcel of the inaudible, the irrepressible melody of life that pervades everything while known only to the rare few. Awareness of it can reveal the seams of things and the nodes of being that almost all of us miss in this contingent phase of existence.

Guy Murchie, *The Seven Mysteries of Life*

Φ

The description of this proportion as Golden or Divine is fitting perhaps because it is seen by many to open the door to a deeper understanding of beauty and spirituality in life. That's an incredible role for one number to play, but then again this one number has played an incredible role in human history and the universe at large.

H.E. Huntley, *The Divine Proportion: A Study in Mathematical Beauty*

Divinely Coded Vitruvian Woman and Man revealing the Universal Divine Code of unity, harmony and genius.

The Golden Ratio is a universal law in which is contained the ground-principle of all formative striving for beauty and completeness in the realms of both nature and art, and which permeates, as a paramount spiritual ideal, all structures, forms and proportions, whether cosmic or individual, organic or inorganic, acoustic or optical; which finds its fullest realization, however, in the human form.

Adolf Zeising, nineteenth century German Golden Ratio researcher & scientist

Introduction

The Master Code Carrier From Pisa

His name was Leonardo Fibonacci of Pisa, and he lived from c. 1178 to 1255. The greatest yet forgotten mathematician of the Middle Ages, he introduced to the West the Hindu/Arabic number system, the name and concept of Zero and the decimal system. Eight centuries ago, Fibonacci also recognized and enumerated the blueprint for the ubiquitous, original code of creation. This code has had many names over the centuries: The Golden Mean, Golden Ratio, Divine Proportion, Golden Section, Extreme and Mean Ratio, etc. We call it the Divine Code. Countless geniuses, such as Da Vinci and Einstein, knew the Code consciously and expressed it in their life and work. Throughout the Universe, energy and matter invariably follow this Code in manifestation, form and function.

If there were such a thing as a "God Code" that blueprints the Universe at every level, the Divine Code would have to be it. Within the realm of man, this pervasive principle underscores all creative endeavors. It underlies successful and fulfilling art, architecture, music, science, medicine, relationships, business, athletic achievement and spirituality. The reason anyone is successful at anything—even though they may not know why or may attribute it to other causes—is that they have accessed and applied Divine Code principles in some way to whatever they think, make or do. The reason we consider anything to be good, true or beautiful is that it awakens and delights our inherent Divine Code nature.

What This Book Uses: The Fractal Power of Quotes

This book features a unique collection of quotes regarding the Divine Code. Most are drawn from our books, *The Divine Code of Da Vinci, Fibonacci, Einstein & YOU* and *The Divine Code Lifestyle Diet.* Each quote is by a genius with his or her own insights into the Divine Code, either directly or in spirit. Quotes are potent activation agents: they are short, concise and to the point. They convey maximal information with minimal words. The information is laser-like, with the ability to penetrate and transform one's consciousness. These quotes are also fractal in nature, in that each quote contains a facet of the Divine Code, and offers its own unique window into its magic. Note: a fractal is simply a small part that reflects a greater whole, like a small piece of broccoli has the same shape or pattern as the whole head.

In the selected quotes throughout this book, the Divine Code is reflected in innumerable fields, including science, geometry, art, architecture, medicine, business, religion, philosophy and health. Another fascinating quality of fractals is their ability to rapidly transmit the essence of a subject, in a most efficient and profound manner. By reading these quotes, one can absorb the essential qualities of the Divine Code in the shortest amount of time. In essence, a few key words can speak volumes and ignite a chain reaction of awakening and insight. The power of these Divine Code quotes resonates to our core, as each of us was designed in both structure and function with the blueprint of the Divine Code in mind. In this spirit, this short book can be an easy and enjoyable way to access the Greatest Secret of the Universe.

The Promise

The promise and power of the Divine Code to activate your personal genius code is now in your hands. You are an extraordinary expression of the Divine Code, with enormous latent genius potential— however successful you may be today. Sometimes our innate genius merely needs a little coaxing—a "jump start"—to ignite it and shift it into gear. You need only to reactivate or catalyze the Divine Code and your genius will then begin to express itself in any area of your life in which it is applied. Art, architecture, science, medicine, health and longevity, finance, relationships or spiritual understanding—the list is as endless as your imagination. Consider yourself in excellent company—that of Pythagoras, Fibonacci, Da Vinci, Pacioli, Kepler, Einstein, Watson, Crick, Wilkins and Franklin—and all of the countless other Divine Code geniuses throughout history. What separates them from you is only one thing. Their Divine Code was activated.

To begin your journey of discovery and activation of your personal genius, along with Leonardo Fibonacci and all of our featured Divine Code Carriers, simply turn the page...

The Divine Code

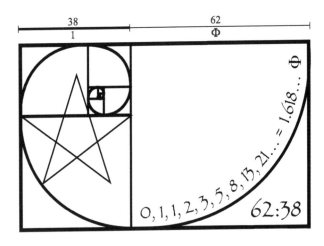

- The infinite Fibonacci Sequence: 0, 1, 1, 2, 3, 5, 8, 13, 21...
- The Golden Ratio of 1.618...
- The Golden Rectangle
- The Golden Spiral
- The Golden Star

O

___

The Secret Code of the Universe: The Divine Code

The Quintessential Divine Code

The Divine Code is fundamentally a profound yet simple ratio of symmetry, efficiency, harmony and success. It speaks of the mysterious, hidden *Quality* of numbers and their relationships vs. just their obvious *Quantities*. It is not necessary to know or learn advanced mathematics to understand or apply the Code; indeed a child can with ease. For those who love math, an extraordinary world awaits. However, this is not a mathematical book. The Divine Code is a simple formula that when applied to anything, always creates greater value, beauty and unity— a greater whole that always exceeds the sum of its parts.

The Divine Code's 5 primary facets are:

- The Fibonacci Sequence: 0, 1, 1, 2, 3, 5, 8, 13, 21...
- The Golden Ratio of 1.618... $\vdash\!\!\frac{62}{\Phi}\!\!\longrightarrow\!\!\frac{38}{1}\!\!\dashv$
- The Golden Rectangle ▭
- The Golden Spiral ℰ
- The Golden Star ☆

One could say that these are 5 integrated aspects of the Code that underlie all creation. This Code can be simply and ingeniously utilized in many ways. It's like rediscovering an "Open Sesame" to a higher order and quality of life. Consider the historical impact and implications of the Divine Code:

- The form and function, the structure and movement of the natural world are based on it.

- It has been a key inspiration for many geniuses throughout history. From Leonardo Fibonacci, to Leonardo Da Vinci, to Albert Einstein, the essence of the Divine Code has been kept alive and passed down through the centuries.

- The secrets of success in health, nutrition, exercise, longevity, wealth and peak performance can be unlocked through its use.

- Relationships and intimacy can be enhanced through its conscious application.

- The keys to greater self-understanding, creativity and spiritual growth are contained within it.

Leonardo Fibonacci

The Fibonacci Sequence & the Golden Ratio

This deceptively simple yet magical Sequence of numbers was introduced in Fibonacci's classic book, *Liber Abaci* (1202) and later named in Fibonacci's honor. The infinite Sequence is formed by adding one number to the next, beginning with zero:

0, 1, 1, 2, 3, 5, 8, 13, 21, 34, 55, 89, 144, 233, 377...

The Golden Ratio or Phi Φ is a special value, closely related to the Fibonacci Sequence. It is in fact the ratio of its successive terms. If you graph the ratios of adjacent numbers in the Sequence, you'll see that they converge on the Golden Ratio: 1.618. The ratios actually "dance" around the Golden Ratio (see Divine Pulse graph), with the first ratio lower than 1.618 and the next ratio higher than 1.618, ad infinitum.

1/1 = **1**	13/8 = **1.625**
2/1 = **2**	21/13 = **1.615**
3/2 = **1.5**	34/21 = **1.619**
5/3 = **1.66**	55/34 = **1.617**
8/5 = **1.6**	89/55 = **1.618...**

This is Nature's way of honing in on the elusive Golden Ratio, which doesn't actually exist in this dimension, as it's an infinite, irrational number. Either way, we arrive at very special numbers: 1.618,

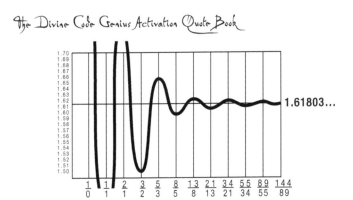

The Divine Pulse Graph: Fibonacci Sequence ratios, forever zeroing-in on the elusive Golden Ratio 1.61803...

or 0.618 if you invert the ratios. Greek mathematicians and architects of Plato's time (c. 400 B.C.) and before recognized this value geometrically, since they didn't express ratios using decimals or Hindu/Arabic numerals. Aesthetically, this proportion was of considerable significance and was used liberally as an integral part of their designs. Two of the more famous examples are the Parthenon in Athens and the Great Pyramid in Egypt.

Bringing the Golden Ratio Down to Earth: The Golden Ratio Fudge Factor

A fast and easy way to avoid intimidating mathematics and still use Golden Ratios in your daily life is to use the Golden Ratio approximations of 62% and 38%—or even more roughly, 60% and 40%. So, if you're filling your wine glass to make the full-to-empty ratio approximate the Golden Ratio, try filling your glass a little less than 40% full. Remember that the other 60% is the complementary unfilled portion that makes up the larger aspect of the Golden Ratio (of course, you could instead fill your glass 60% full). Eyeballing is an easy, non-scientific way to use the fudge factor and to develop your inner sense of Divine Proportion. This simple technique of Golden Ratio approximation can be used with any system of measure—including volume, distance, time or weight, to easily reap the benefits of working with the Golden Ratio.

Another common example of the use of a fudge factor is in computer graphics programs, where a function called "snap-to" is used to automatically place text or graphics in alignment with column or margin guides. In such programs, as you're aligning text or graphics, they automatically click into place when they get close enough to the margin or column. Likewise, when moving a file on your desktop into an icon on your dock, the file will click into place when it gets reasonably close to the destination. This fudge factor is built-in to the computer program, just as anything getting reasonably close to the Golden Ratio is subjected to its gravitational pull and "snaps-to" its place.

Even the great Leonardo Da Vinci apparently used the Golden Ratio fudge factor in his rendering of *The Vitruvian Man*. An interesting analysis at www.world-mysteries.com/sci_17_vm.htm, shows that the ratio Leonardo used to divide *The Vitruvian Man's* height at the navel, from head to toe, was 1.656—just .0038 away from the Golden Ratio of 1.618. Da Vinci was no doubt counting on the fact that our brains have a built-in Golden Ratio fudge factor that will "snap-to,"

MONTH							
ONE 1 pair	🐰🐰						
TWO 1 pair	🐰🐰						
THREE 2 pairs	🐰🐰 🐰🐰						
FOUR 3 pairs	🐰🐰 🐰🐰 🐰🐰						
FIVE 5 pairs	🐰🐰 🐰🐰 🐰🐰 🐰🐰 🐰🐰						
SIX 8 pairs	🐰🐰 🐰🐰 🐰🐰 🐰🐰 🐰🐰 🐰🐰 🐰🐰 🐰🐰						
SEVEN 13 pairs	🐰🐰 🐰🐰 🐰🐰 🐰🐰 🐰🐰 🐰🐰 🐰🐰 🐰🐰 🐰🐰 🐰🐰 🐰🐰 🐰🐰 🐰🐰						
EIGHT 21 pairs	🐰🐰 🐰🐰						

The beginning of Fibonacci's "Rabbit Riddle,"
which introduced the Fibonacci Sequence.

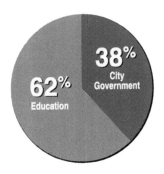

38/62 Golden Ratio
pie graph.

Glass 62% full.

when given a close approximation of the Golden Ratio. Likewise, we can take advantage of our brain's innate Golden Ratio programming and not feel off-base if our use of the Golden Ratio is approximated or hinted at, yet not exact or perfect.

While perfect is both the target and the magnet, getting within the range of perfect—reaching excellence vs. perfection—is close enough. Remember that we can never actually reach the perfect Golden Ratio anyway—it is an abstract, infinite ideal. At best, we can only very closely approximate it. This is why there's an infinite ellipse at the end of the numerical expression of the Golden Ratio: 1.6180339... In essence, the Golden Ratio as far as can be mathematically represented is in itself an infinite fudge-factor. It is a non-repeating, irrational number that never actually "reaches" the exact Golden Ratio—it is seemingly impossible, at least in the material dimension. Yet Nature and Man are ever-striving for the ideal in form, function and growth, with the Golden Ratio as our bright, magnetic North Star. It is our innate evolutionary impulse, the never-ending striving towards perfection, which the Golden Ratio represents.

The Golden Rectangle

The Golden Rectangle has a ratio of length to width of 1.618 (and width to length of 0.618). Ancient Greek architects beautifully embedded Golden Rectangles in the construction of the classic Parthenon, a source of attraction and fascination for millennia. The Golden Rectangle has the ability to recreate itself an infinite

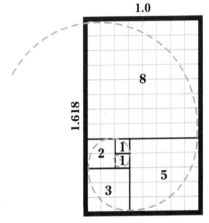

Golden Ratio Rectangle (1.618:1.0), from which a Golden Spiral can also be created. Note how the Fibonacci Sequence numbers guide the literal building blocks for every Golden Rectangle, including the 8" x 5" cover of this book (8/5 =1.6).

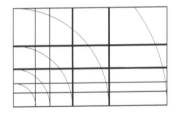

(*clockwise starting upper left*) Golden Ratio design GRiD and three classic Golden Rectangle examples: the Parthenon, a Credit Card, a Flag.

number of times on an infinite number of levels, large and small. Simply by adding a square that fits the long side of any existing Golden Rectangle, a larger Golden Rectangle can be created. Conversely, by removing a square from an existing Golden Rectangle, a smaller Golden Rectangle can be created. This process of fractal self-similarity can continue indefinitely in both directions. Such a rectangle will always maintain the proportions of the Divine Code, no matter the scale. We could say that the Golden Rectangle is the linear male aspect of the Golden Ratio and the Golden Spiral is the curvaceous, feminine aspect.

Golden & Fibonacci Spirals

Golden and Fibonacci Spirals are abundantly found at all levels of creation including spiral galaxies, ocean wave curls, seashells, hurricane swirls, ram's

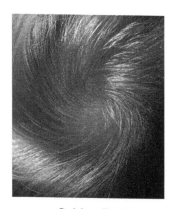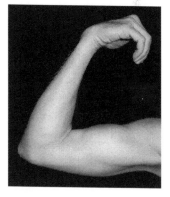

Golden Ratio spiral hair pattern on top of child's head and linear representation of Fibonacci spiral in fingers, hand, forearm, upper arm.

horns and in the spirals on the scales of pineapples and pinecones. They are also visible in swirling hair patterns on the top of our heads and in the way our fingers and arms curl and uncurl. Everywhere we look, Nature seems to delight in using Golden and Fibonacci Spirals as the basis for her creation's design, structure and function. While Golden Spirals and Fibonacci Spirals look very similar, they have some differences.

- A Golden Spiral is a type of ideal logarithmic spiral that always grows larger by a factor of approximately 1.618 per turn. The Golden Spiral has a constant ratio of growth (or regress) at the large and the small ends of the spiral.

(clockwise starting upper left) Four classic examples of Nature's Golden Spirals: Nautilus Shell, Ocean Wave, Galaxy, Ram's Horn.

- A Fibonacci Spiral on the other hand, appears very similar to a Golden Spiral at its large expanding end, but has changing ratios (from the Fibonacci Sequence) at its small or contracting end (1, 2, 1.5, 1.66, 1.6, 1.625, 1.615, 1.619, 1.617...)

The two spirals—the Golden and the Fibonacci—are therefore fundamentally different. In our physical dimension, the Golden Ratio and Spiral are Divine Ideals for which we can only imagine and strive. Nature hints at these infinite Golden Ratios and Spirals by practically using Fibonacci Ratios and Spirals.

The Golden Star

Whenever you draw a simple five-pointed star, or pentagram, the lines are always automatically and precisely cut into Golden Ratio segments. The familiar pattern of the Golden Star is instantly recognized in the shapes of starfish and five-petaled flowers. The Golden Star can be easily superimposed over a silhouette of a human being, arms and legs outstretched. In addition,

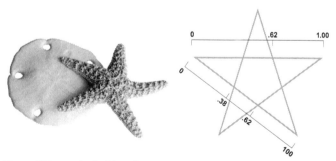

Two of Nature's Golden Stars, in a Sand Dollar and Starfish, along with a Pentagram with Golden Ratio cuts.

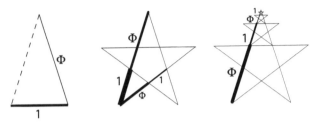

Golden Ratio fractal growth pattern of the common
5-pointed star pentagram.

the Golden Star also shares a remarkable ability
with the Fibonacci Sequence, the Golden Rectangle
and the Golden Spiral: it can grow exponentially from
within itself. Integral theorist Stephen McIntosh points
out that:

> *The initial division of the line in Phi proportion is the*
> *genesis of the ubiquitous five-pointed star. The star is a*
> *fundamental diagram of the self-similarity used by the*
> *life force to grow from within it. This self-generating*
> *pattern is one of evolution's techniques of creation.*

The pentagram is also a universally recognized
symbol of brilliance, excellence and success. It has been
in use since ancient times, from pre-history cultures
to Pythagoreans and Pagans, who all understood its
meaning and power. The Golden Star provides the
opportunity to access the power of the Divine Code
simply by gazing at it and appreciating the timeless,
open secret that it carries. As Dan Brown notes in
The Da Vinci Code:

> *The ratios of the line segments in the pentacle [the*
> *five-pointed, Golden Star] all equal PHI, making this*

symbol the ultimate symbol of the Divine Proportion. For this reason, the five-pointed star has always been a symbol of beauty and perfection associated with the Goddess and the sacred feminine.

Raymond Buckhead, author of *The Witches Book,* adds this intriguing insight into the power of the Golden Star:

The Pentagram... is designed to facilitate the acquisition of all secret knowledge.

Every rose contains a double imprint of the Divine Code: petals embedded in Golden Spirals on the front and a five-pointed Golden Star on the back.

1a

The Universal Genius Activation Code

Exposure to any aspect or facet of the Divine Code has the potential to catalyze and activate the unique genius inherent in every person. No matter what your chosen field or endeavor, a quantum jump in insight and success is likely to happen as a result of exposure to the Code. Prominent examples of this include Leonardo Fibonacci, Fra Luca Pacioli, Leonardo Da Vinci and Albert Einstein. A review of the biographies of these and many other history-shaping individuals reveals that they all had one unusual thing in common. At some point in their lives, often early on, they learned of the Divine Code. This learning occurred in many ways, such as through reading a textbook on sacred geometry, being instructed by a mentor, or via observation and contemplation of the Divine patterns and rhythms in Nature. Once the Divine Code activation occurred for these individuals, they went on to make great discoveries and contributions in their particular fields. The same possibility awaits you now.

Leonardo Fibonacci (c. 1178-1255):
Master of the Divine Code

A prime example is the great, yet unheralded, Leonardo Fibonacci. Fibonacci (c. 1178-1255) contributed four monumental achievements to the world. He introduced to Western civilization the Hindu/Arabic numerals (1,2,3...), the concept of zero and the decimal system. His fourth great achievement was the elaboration of the "rabbit riddle," which was based on what was later to be known as the "Fibonacci Sequence." These advances radically changed Western science, business, art and architecture. They laid the foundation for the Renaissance and set the stage for the world we live in today. What turned Fibonacci into "The One" who would share these ground-breaking insights with the West? Earlier in his life and travels he was exposed to the Golden Ratio in the works of Greek and Arab scholars, i.e. Euclid and Al-Kwarizmi, among others. At first, this might simply seem like a curious coincidence. However, exposure to the Golden Ratio and the

Divine Code appears to have a great and mysterious power to open, expand and unlock one's consciousness and activate higher potentials and hidden talents.

Leonardo Da Vinci (1452-1519) and his mentor, Fra Luca Pacioli (1445-1517)

The legendary Fra Luca Pacioli instructed Leonardo Da Vinci in Divine Proportion and artistic perspective. Pacioli, a sacred geometry master, initiated Da Vinci into the mysteries and endless applications of the Divine Code. After this period of exposure to the principles of the Code, many of Da Vinci's works often directly expressed aspects of the Golden Ratio, including the world's most well known painting, the Mona Lisa. Da Vinci's visionary expressions as a scientist and artist were likely catalyzed by his early exposure to the Code, as taught by his mentor Fra Luca Pacioli. Pacioli immersed himself in the study of the Divine Code to such a degree that he was known as "the monk drunk

Leonardo Da Vinci. Fra Luca Pacioli.

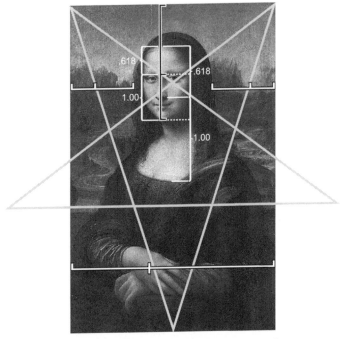

Multiple Golden Ratios in the world's most famous painting, Leonardo Da Vinci's *Mona Lisa* (1503-1507).

on beauty." Beauty of course is simply the Divine Code expressed by Nature in her innumerable stunning forms.

After his own Divine Code awakening, Pacioli went on to write not only his famous De Divina Proportione, he also wrote the earliest book on double entry accounting, Summa de Arithmetica, Geometrica, Proportioni et Proportionalita (The Summation of Arithmetic, Geometry, Proportion and Proportionality). Pacioli's insights and work are the foundation of all accounting and business systems in use around the world to this

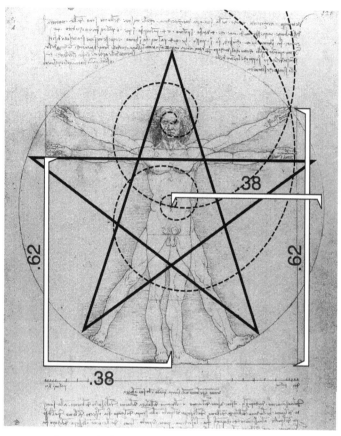

Leonardo Da Vinci's *Vitruvian Man* (1487),
showing several prominent Golden Ratios.

day. As a result of this monumental contribution to the
world, Pacioli had another title bestowed upon him—
The Father of Accounting. The insight and genius
necessary to delineate the cornerstones of accounting
was very likely catalyzed by Pacioli's early exposure
and lifelong fascination with the Divine Code.

Einstein & The DNA Pioneers: Watson, Crick, Franklin & Wilkins

Divine Code genius Albert Einstein.

Another fascinating example is Albert Einstein. Einstein was exposed to a "Holy Geometry" book at age 12, where he first learned of the Divine Code and its infinite Fibonacci Sequence. Einstein subsequently went on to elaborate his Theory of Relativity, forever changing the world in the process. Einstein's Nobel-prize winning discoveries may have had little directly to do with the Divine Code. However, clearly something very potent had happened to Einstein as a boy to open his awareness to be able to recognize and formulate his great theories, including his world-famous Theory of Relativity, $E=mc^2$. Einstein had been initiated into the genius realm by his early exposure to the Divine Code.

Many other geniuses have been exposed to the Code directly, yet did not consciously recognize its profound nature. The Code nevertheless had immense impact on their work and lives. A prime example of this type of exposure is the case of the popular discoverers of DNA, James Watson, Francis Crick, Maurice Wilkins—and the forgotten Rosalind Franklin. All were constantly enveloped by the ever-present Divine Proportions of DNA's double-helical structure. Yet they probably

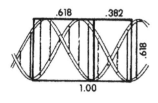 

L: DNA with Golden Ratios. *R*: Einstein's E=mc^2
sculpture (2006) in Berlin, Germany.

didn't realize that the length-to-width ratio of DNA was in Golden Ratio. However, merely by working with the molecule itself, their brains were supercharged and the flash of insight necessary to determine the structure of DNA occurred. They were directly in contact with a prototypical example of the Golden Ratio, yet likely didn't realize it. The effect that the Ratio had on them was oblique and unconscious. However, the results were of Nobel-prize winning and world-changing caliber.

Your Divine Code genius activation quotes begin in the next section. As Leonardo Fibonacci might say, *Buona Fortuna!*

The Divine Code Genius Activation Quote Book

The Divine Code Genius Activation Quotes

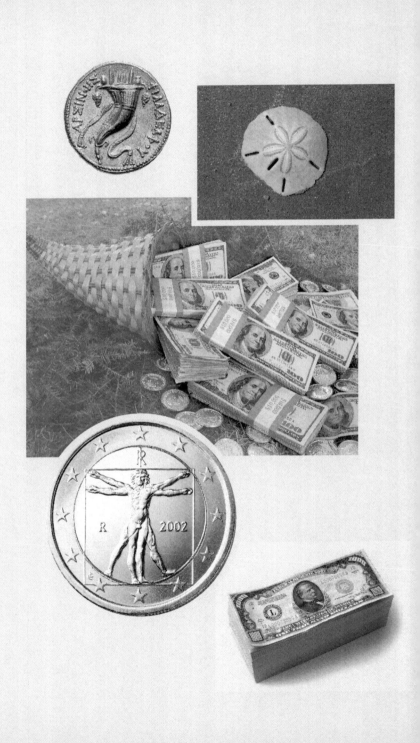

1b

Abundance & Business

The great Golden Spiral seems to be Nature's way of building quantity, without sacrificing quality.

William Hoffer, author, *Midnight Express* and *Not Without My Daughter*

Good fortune follows the Divine Code.

Matthew Cross

In these two crucial ways (Fibonacci and spiraling), the sociological valuation of man's productive enterprise [the stock market] reflects other growth forms found throughout nature. We conclude, therefore, they all follow the same law.

Robert R. Prechter, Jr., ElliottWave.com

We need a transformation to a new economics of win-win cooperation where everyone comes out better. There will still be inequalities; some people will win more than others, but everyone will gain. Everybody loses under the system that nourishes win-lose thinking...

Dr. W. Edwards Deming, the Einstein
of Quality and Success

Whoever cultivates the Golden Mean avoids both the poverty of a hovel and the envy of a palace.

Horace, ancient Roman poet

What is out of ratio in your business or life today, but if it were in more harmonious ratio, it would fundamentally change your business and life for the better?

Matthew Cross and Robert Friedman, M.D.'s Key
Paradigm Transformation Question, inspired by the
pioneering work of Futurist Joel Barker, author of
Paradigms: The Business of Discovering The Future.
JoelBarker.com

...the guidance system that is within you is there to show you the Path of Least Resistance. It is there to show you your Path of Allowing your connection to Source Energy. This guidance system is so present, and so particular and so direct, so in the moment, so on the mark... it is the path to all you seek. It's the path to your source; it's the path to your wellness; it's the path to everything you've ever asked for...

Abraham, Abraham-Hicks.com

He that holds fast the Golden Mean, and lives contently between the little and the great, feels not the wants that pinch the poor, nor plagues that haunt the rich man's door.

William Cowper, English poet

Power is being able to have the courage to do what you love.

Anastasia Soare, Hollywood's Golden Ratio natural beauty expert

Lack of time is actually lack of priorities. Being selective— doing less—is the path of the productive.

Timothy Ferriss, *The Four Hour Workweek*
FourHourWorkWeek.com

Anyone can be more effective with less effort by learning how to identify and leverage the 80/20 principle—the well-known, unpublicized secret that 80 percent of all our results in business and in life stem from a mere 20 percent of our efforts.

Richard Koch, *The 80/20 Principle*
[a.k.a. the Pareto Principle]

2

Beauty

The good, of course, is always beautiful, and the beautiful never lacks proportion.

Plato, Greek philosopher

Beauty is not "Perfection." Real beauty is Proportion.

Anastasia Soare, Hollywood's Golden Ratio natural beauty expert

...it can be said that wherever there is an intensification of function or a particular beauty and harmony of form, there the Golden Mean will be found.

Robert Lawlor, sacred geometer and author, *Sacred Geometry: Philosophy and Practice*

Every beauty which is seen here by persons of perception resembles more than anything else that celestial source from which we all come.

Michelangelo, Renaissance artist

The beauty of one form is akin to the beauty of another, and that beauty in every form is one and the same.

Plato, Greek philosopher

The beautiful is a manifestation of the secret laws of Nature. When Nature begins to reveal her open secret to a person, she feels an irresistible longing for her most worthy interpreter, ART.

Johann Wolfgang von Goethe, luminary German writer and polymath

All beauty is mathematics.

Ancient Greeks

I became really obsessed with the eyebrow, because nobody thought it was important... Taking all the knowledge I learned from Da Vinci and Fibonacci, I was able to get at the perfect Golden Proportion on anybody's face. Even when features are asymmetrical—as they often are—well-shaped brows will bring harmony, proportion and balance to the face.

Anastasia Soare, Hollywood's Golden Ratio natural beauty expert

If the Golden Ratio makes the front of a building look fantastic, imagine what it can do for the backside of a woman.

    Vogue Magazine, April 2007; *The Proportion of Blu* (designer jean company, whose fit is based on the Golden Ratio).

An Archives of Sexual Behavior study reveals that woman are most attracted to muscular men whose shoulders measure 1.6 times [the Golden Ratio] the size of their waist.

    John Barban, *The Perfect Body Formula*; *Men's Health* Magazine, July/August 2008

The Fashion Code is based on the timeless secret for beauty [the Divine Proportion] that has inspired everyone from Da Vinci to today's top fashion icons. Once women know what this secret is and how to use it, they will have the power to create the perfect outfit everyday.

    Sara and Ruth Levy, developers of *The Fashion Code*

The Divine Proportion is Nature's yardstick for beauty.

    Ruth Levy, co-developer of *The Fashion Code*

It's [the Divine Proportion-based Fashion Code] a real jaw-dropper... I'm a believer!...

    Rachel Ray, commenting on the live presentation on her popular talk show of Sara and Ruth Levy's *Fashion Code.*

In all cultures, people judged beautiful have bodies that exhibit the Divine Proportion, or Golden Ratio, of 1 to 1.618. In beautiful humans, the Golden Ratio turns up all over: in the distance between the eyes relative to the length of the lower face, the height of a front tooth relative to the width of both front teeth, the length of the arms relative to body height...

Martha Beck, *Makeover Madness* from *O*,
the *Oprah* Magazine: April 15, 2005

The theory is that the more symmetrical a face is, the healthier it is... the formula for beauty is that precise golden ratio (go ahead and pull a ruler and a calculator on your next date). The [Golden] ratio holds for the width of the cheekbones to the width of the mouth... [similarly] the width of the mouth should be roughly 1.6 times the width of the bottom of the nose... Scientists also believe that symmetry is equated with a strong immune system— indicating that more robust genes make a person more attractive. Of course, that's the element of beauty that you typically can't control. You have what you were born with. But that doesn't mean that you can't make changes—changes to enhance your beauty and, along with it, the way you feel about yourself.

Dr. Mehmet Oz, co-author of the popular *YOU: The Owner's Manual* health book series and one of *Time* magazine's "100 Most Influential People" (2008) and *Esquire* magazine's 75 Most Influential People of the 21st Century

3

Art, Design & Architecture

I learned about the basic 'Rule of Thirds' in design school, without the clear 'why' behind the principle. It always seemed to add a general dynamic element to the layout and presentation of data and images. Before learning about the Divine Code, I used the Rule of Thirds often, as a balancing element for the approximate spacing of things within a design layout... Now, I look for more and deeper ways to directly, consciously embed the more exact 62:38 Golden Ratio in my work. I'm looking for opportunities to relate various elements of a design back to the whole overall design, to create a 'greater, more appealing whole, which exceeds the sum of its parts.'

Tom Reczek, Divine Code Designer;
618Design.com

All of creation expresses itself through number—and number is frequency, manifest as color, sound and form, and even as emotion and states of consciousness. The effects of harmonious design [and music] based on sacred proportions can be experienced first hand when one enters an ancient temple in Egypt or a Gothic cathedral, such as Chartres. The effect can be immediately sensed as harmonious, powerful and centering, and being inside a space [or listening to music] designed with sacred proportions helps us to access other dimensions of consciousness...

> Ani Williams, founder of Songaia Sound
> AniWilliams.com

I call architecture frozen music.

> Johann Wolfgang Von Goethe, luminary German writer and polymath

Renaissance artists regularly used the Golden Section in dividing the surface of a painting into pleasing proportions, just as architects naturally used it to analyze the proportions of a building.

> Matila Ghyka; Romanian mathematician, aristocrat and author, *The Geometry of Art and Life*

Design is not just what it looks like and feels like. Design is how it works.

> Steven P. Jobs, Cofounder & CEO of Apple Inc.

Phidias, the Greek sculptor, revealed the Golden Ratio in his work—for example, in such proportions as the relation of the width of the head to the width of the throat, the width of the forearm to the wrist, the width of the calf to the ankle, and so on.

James Wyckoff, *Pyramid Power*

The Golden Ratio... is of substantial importance to Masons.

Jeremy Harwood, *The Freemasons*

[Thomas Jefferson] believed that the elegant proportions of ancient structures would evoke the chief values of the Enlightenment: reason, order, and freedom. 'Embellished with Athenian taste,' he declared, the [U.S.] capitol building would become 'the first temple dedicated to the sovereignty of the people.'

Trevor Howells, editor/author of
The World's Greatest Buildings

The largest isosceles triangle of the ancient Hindu Sri Yantra mandala design is one of the face triangles of the Great Pyramid in miniature. It reveals almost exactly the same relationship between pi and phi as in its larger, Great Pyramid counterpart.

George Joseph, *The Crest of the Peacock*

The Ancients, having taken into consideration the rigorous construction of the human body, elaborated all their works, as especially their holy temples, according to these proportions; for they found here the two principal figures without which no project is possible: the perfection of the circle, the principle of all regular bodies, and the equilateral square.

Fra Luca Pacioli, Da Vinci's mentor
and the "Father of Accounting"

I constantly tried Fibonacci sequences on occasion to shorten programs. For example, if I needed a program that generated a specific sequence I might try the Fibonacci sequence, modulo some constant and see if the finite sequence I needed came out. I searched everywhere for any trick that saved code...

Stephen Wozniak, Cofounder of Apple Inc.

Without mathematics there is no art.

Fra Luca Pacioli, Da Vinci's mentor
and the "Father of Accounting"

Phi... had supposedly been first discovered by the Pythagorean Greeks, who incorporated it into the Parthenon at Athens. There is absolutely no doubt, however, that phi was illustrated and obtained at least 2000 years previously in the King's Chamber [and master blueprint] of the Great Pyramid at Giza.

Graham Hancock, *Fingerprints of the Gods*

Thomas Jefferson's scheme for the University Rotunda [library] takes a novel curvilinear approach that appears to utilize the "extreme and mean" ratio with originality and vigor. There is, in this masterwork of proportion, a freedom of expression that reflects the youth and vitality of America's revolutionary spirit, as Jefferson reinvents classical forms through techniques of his own creation.

Rachel Fletcher, geometer and museum curator, *An American Vision of Harmony: Geometric Proportions in Thomas Jefferson's Rotunda at the University of Virginia*

Obama's overly large signature shows he likes attention and is a bit of an egotist. Interestingly, whether he did it consciously or subconsciously, by intersecting the "O" and the "b" in his last name, Obama formed the Greek symbol, known as "Phi." "Phi" represents the golden ratio or section – the "ideal" proportion recognized by mathematicians, artists and architects since ancient times.

Michelle Dresbold, hand writing analyst, on U.S. President Barack Obama's signature

There is a geometry of art as there is a geometry of life, and, as the Greeks had guessed, they happen to be the same.

Matila Ghyka; Romanian mathematician, aristocrat and author, *The Geometry of Art and Life*

To the sculptors of classical Greece and Rome, the Divine Proportion was recognized as ideal for the human anatomy.

Bulent Atalay, *Math and The Mona Lisa*

...The instinct for art is innate. First, one has to love nature with all one's heart and soul, and be able to study and admire it for hours on end. Everything is in nature. A plant, a leaf, a blade of grass should be the subjects of infinite and fruitful meditations; for the artist, a cloud floating in the sky has form, and the form affords him joy, helps him think.

William Adolphe Bouguereau, French painter

Ever since I was a little boy, I would study composition. And it was [Divine Code composer] Tchaikovsky that influenced me the most.

Michael Jackson, in *Ebony* Magazine;
December, 2007

Michael Jackson loved art and studied Michelangelo and Da Vinci.

Nate Giorgio, master artist who worked extensively with Michael Jackson

The true work of art is but a shadow of the divine perfection.

Michelangelo, Renaissance artist

5

Fractals

Fractal, n: A small part of a whole which has the same pattern or shape of the whole, like a piece of broccoli retains the shape of the whole broccoli head. This property, also called self-similarity, as at work at every scale in the Universe, from the micro to the macro. Each fractal–regardless of scale–is essentially a reduced size copy of the whole, like a hologram, e.g., it could be said that humans are fractals of God. The ubiquitous Divine Code is a prime fractal example. The term was coined by the Polish-born French-US mathematician Benoît Mandelbrot (1924-) from the Latin fractus, "to break" [into self-similar pieces].

Definition by Matthew Cross

If we wish to understand the nature of the Universe, we have an inner hidden advantage; we are ourselves are little portions of the Universe and so carry the answer within us.

Ronald David Laing, Scottish psychiatrist

The initial division of a line in Phi proportion is the genesis of the ubiquitous five-pointed star. The star is a fundamental diagram of the self-similarity used by the life force to grow from within it. This self-generating pattern is one of evolution's techniques of creation.

Stephen Ian McIntosh, Integral theorist and author, *Integral Consciousness and the Future of Evolution*

Man is all symmetry, full of proportions, one limb to another, and all to all the world besides. Each part may call the farthest brother, for head with foot hath private amity, and both with moons and tides.

George Herbert
English priest and poet

I'm just intrigued with the beauty between the major and the minor chord, and the challenge of creating something magic that is outside me and inside me, too.

Annie Lennox, pioneering singer/songwriter, Eurythmics co-founder and fan of Divine Code composer Claude Debussy

There is a code that lies both within and without. This secret yet open code points the way to your purpose, your happiness and your greatness... it goes by the name of The Divine Code.

Matthew Cross

The flapping of a butterfly's wings can trouble a star.

Ancient Sufi saying

I discovered the secret of the sea in meditation upon the dewdrop.

Kahlil Gibran: Lebanese American artist and writer

Through the science of Fractal Cognition™, it is possible to convey vast amounts of information, indeed the essence of any subject, via a meaningful small part or fractal. Like the spiral shape of a Nautilus shell mirrors the great spiral galaxies in the heavens, or a tiny broccoli flowerette mirrors the shape of a whole head of broccoli, this principle is at work everywhere at every scale in the Universe.

Matthew Cross

The essential feature of quantum interconnectedness is that the whole universe is enfolded in everything, and that each thing is enfolded in the whole.

David Bohm, Noble Prize-winning physicist and colleague of Einstein

The Pentagram... is considered to symbolize microcosmic man... man as a microcosm of the Universe, superimposed on a 5-pointed star... an illustration of the principle "as above, so below..."

Raymond Buckhead, *The Witches Book*

It's as though we are somehow programmed by mathematics. Seashell, galaxy, snowflake or human: we're all bound by the same order... [and] because man is subject to rhythmical procedure, calculations having to do with his activities can be projected far into the future with a justification and certainty heretofore unattainable.

Ralph Nelson Elliott, formulator of the
Wave Principle of stock market movements

Even as the finite encloses an infinite series,
And in the unlimited limits appear,
So the soul of immensity dwells in minutia,
And in the narrowest limits no limit in here.
What joy to discern the minute in infinity,
The vast to perceive in the small, what divinity!

Jakob Bernoulli, mathematician
and probability theory pioneer

I ask you to look both ways. For the road to a knowledge of the stars leads through the atom; and the important knowledge of the atom has been reached through the stars.

Sir Arthur Eddington, 20th-century
British astrophysicist

Each time a man stands up for an ideal... he sends forth a tiny ripple of hope, and crossing each other from a million different centers of energy and daring, those ripples build a current that can sweep down the mightiest walls of oppression and resistance....

Robert F. Kennedy, U.S. Senator & statesman
South Africa, 1966

If you do right in the upstream, the downstream will be much easier.

Teruaki Aoki, Vice President at Sony

85% of the results from any endeavor are in the First 15% of the process.

Dr. W. Edwards Deming, the Einstein
of Quality and Success, attributed

Leonardo envisaged the great picture chart of the human body he had produced through his anatomical drawings and Vitruvian Man as a cosmografia del minor mondo (cosmography of the microcosm). He believed the workings of the human body to be an analogy for the workings of the universe.

Encyclopaedia Britannica online,
on Leonardo Da Vinci

The shell, like the creature within it, grows in size but does not change in shape; and the existence of this constant relativity of growth [the Golden Spiral], or constant similarity of form, is of the essence.

Sir D'Arcy W. Thompson, English naturalist

To see a world in a grain of sand; and heaven in a wild flower; hold infinity in the palm of your hand; and eternity in an hour.

William Blake, from *Auguries of Innocence*

William Blake said he could see, Vistas of infinity; In the smallest speck of sand, Held in the hollow of his hand; Models for this claim we've got, In the work of Mandelbrot; Fractal diagrams partake, Of the essence sensed by Blake; Basic forms will still prevail, Independent of the Scale; Viewed from far or viewed from near, Special signatures are clear; When you magnify a spot, What you had before, you've got; Smaller, smaller, smaller, yet, Still the same details are set; Finer than the finest hair, Blake's infinity is there; Rich in structure all the way, Just as the mystic poets say.

Professor Jasper Memory, *Blake and Fractals*, from *Mathematics* Magazine

Each person can make a difference and every person should try.

John F. Kennedy, U.S. President

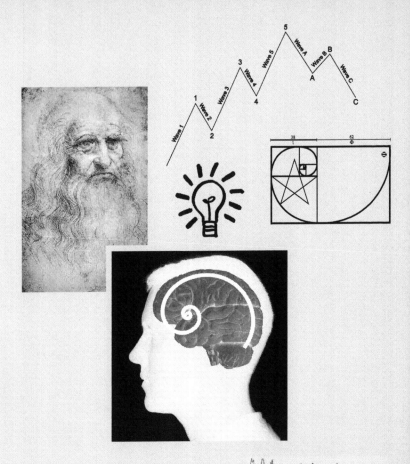
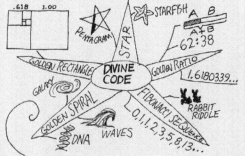

8

Genius Activation & Learning

Discovery consists of seeing what everybody has seen and thinking what nobody has thought.

Albert Szent-Gyorgi, Nobel Laureate
and discoverer of Vitamin C

...the Golden Ratio has inspired thinkers of all disciplines like no other number in the history of mathematics.

Mario Livio, author, *The Golden Ratio: The Story of Phi, The World's Most Astonishing Number*

Imagination is more important than knowledge. I never made any of my most important discoveries through the process of rational thinking alone.

Albert Einstein, Nobel Prize-winning über-genius

[The universe] cannot be read until we have learnt the language and become familiar with the characters in which it is written. It is written in mathematical language, and the letters are triangles, circles and other geometrical figures, without which means it is humanly impossible to comprehend a single word.

Galileo Galilei, pioneering astronomer & scientist

The Golden Section… is a revelation fit to open the kind of fresh, incisive insight into the hidden heart of our universe that thrilled, and would again thrill, Pythagoras and Plato [and Da Vinci] and Copernicus and Kepler and Newton and Einstein. For it is part of the real music of the spheres, parcel of the inaudible, the irrepressible melody of life that pervades everything while known only to the rare few. Awareness of it can reveal the seams of things and the nodes of being that almost all of us miss in this contingent phase of existence.

Guy Murchie, *The Seven Mysteries of Life*

The description of this proportion as Golden or Divine is fitting perhaps because it is seen by many to open the door to a deeper understanding of beauty and spirituality in life. That's an incredible role for one number to play, but then again this one number has played an incredible role in human history and the universe at large.

H.E. Huntley, *The Divine Proportion: A Study in Mathematical Beauty*

The Pentagram... is designed to facilitate the acquisition of all secret knowledge.

Raymond Buckhead, *The Witches Book*

Mathematics seems to endow one with something like a new sense.

Charles Darwin, English naturalist

The real voyage of discovery consists not in seeking new lands but in seeing with new eyes.

Marcel Proust, French novelist

If I have seen further, it is by standing on the shoulders of giants.

Sir Isaac Newton, English physicist & polymath

I recognize that many physicists are smarter than I am—most of them theoretical physicists. A lot of smart people have gone into theoretical physics; therefore the field is extremely competitive. I console myself with the thought that although they may be smarter and may be deeper thinkers than I am, I have broader interests than they have.

Dr. Linus Pauling, acclaimed Vitamin C researcher, and the only double Nobel Prize winner in history (Peace and Chemistry)

A genius is someone who's genes... are suddenly activated by something...

Dr. Kazuo Murakami, DNA scientist and author,
The Divine Code of Life

When my first wife and I began the school [Summerhill], we had one main idea: to make the school fit the child instead of making the child fit the school... Obviously, a school that makes active children sit at desks studying mostly useless subjects is a bad school. It is a good school only for those who believe in such a school, for those uncreative citizens who want docile, uncreative children who will fit into a civilization whose standard of success is money.

A.S. Neill, Author of *Summerhill: A Radical Approach to Child Rearing*

...(Sir Isaac) Newton, who laid the foundations of modern cosmology, was also one of the last of the scholars of the old tradition who accepted that the standards of ancient science were higher than the modern, and sought, like Pythagoras, to rediscover the ancients' knowledge.

John Michell, *The New View Over Atlantis*

The Roma (Gypsies) refer to the pentagram as the star of knowledge.

Victoria Crouch, AncientSpirals.com

When power leads men toward arrogance, poetry reminds him of his limitations. When power narrows the areas of man's concern, poetry reminds him of the richness and diversity of his existence. When power corrupts, poetry cleanses. For art establishes the basic human truth, which must serve as the touchstone of our judgment.

John F. Kennedy, U.S. President

You must understand that it is not only possible, but highly desirable, to do several things simultaneously; thus, it happened that I was operating an international airline, importing thousands of live wild animals, producing films for television and building exercise machines all at the same time. In my opinion, many of our current problems are direct results of specialization; which is why the scientific community has now degenerated to the point of being a sick joke.

Arthur Jones, founder of Nautilus
and the MedX System

My motto is 'there's no future in specialization.'

Karla DeVito, singer, songwriter, actress;
wife of actor Robby Benson

I saw an angel in the stone, and carved to set it free…

Michaelangelo, Renaissance artist,
referring to his Divinely-Coded *David*

A brain listening to music is also a happy brain, and one that enhances learning. University of California, Irvine, researchers found that people who listened to Mozart before taking a pattern-recognition test improved 62 percent [the Golden Ratio] after two days of practice...

Mark Hendricks, *Grey Matters, Entrepreneur Magazine*, January 2006

It should be possible by means of pure deduction to find the picture—that is, the theory—of every natural process, including those of living organisms.

Albert Einstein, Nobel Prize-winning über-genius

If the doors of perception were cleansed, everything would appear to man as it is, infinite.

William Blake, English poet; this passage was
the inspiration for the name of the musical group
The Doors

The most beautiful thing we can experience is the mysterious. It is the source of all true art and science.

Albert Einstein, Nobel Prize-winning über-genius

It's all about Pattern Recognition, about Connecting the Dots...

Arthur J. Samberg, founder of Pequot Capital,
when asked about his secret to success

Don't keep forever on the public road, going only where others have gone. Leave the beaten track occasionally and dive into the woods. You will be certain to find something you have never seen before. It will be a little thing, but do not ignore it; one discovery will lead to another, and before you know it you will have something worth thinking about.

Alexander Graham Bell, inventor

Obstacles cannot crush me. Every obstacle yields to stern resolve. He who is fixed on a star does not change his mind.

Leonardo Da Vinci, the original Renaissance Man

You have learned much Siddhartha. There still remains much to learn. We are not going in circles, we are going upwards. The path is spiral: we have already climbed many steps.

Herman Hesse, *Siddhartha*

Every now and then go away, have a little relaxation, for when you come back to your work your judgment will be surer. Go some distance away because then the work appears smaller and more of it can be taken in at a glance and a lack of harmony and proportion is more readily seen.

Leonardo Da Vinci, the original Renaissance Man

...[True] teaching is nothing like painting, where, by the addition of material to a surface, an image is synthetically produced, but more like the art of sculpture, where, by the subtraction of material, an image already locked in the stone is enabled to emerge. It is a crucial distinction. In other words, I dropped the idea that I was an expert, whose job it was to fill the little heads with my expertise, and began to explore how I could remove those obstacles that prevented the inherent genius of children from gathering itself.

John Taylor Gatto, *Dumbing Us Down*

Real mathematics is not crunching numbers but contemplating them, and the mystery of their connections.

Charles Krauthammer, American Pulitzer Prize-winning columnist

I learned about the Golden Mean when I was about five years old... it greatly fascinated me.

Dr. Murray Gell-Mann, world-renowned physicist, Nobel Prize winner and author, *The Quark and the Jaguar*

The world is but a canvas to our imagination.

Henry David Thoreau, American author (*Walden*)

Perfection is achieved, not when there is nothing left to add, but when there is nothing left to take away.

Antoine de Saint Exupery, French writer and aviator

Make everything as simple as possible, but not simpler.

Albert Einstein, Nobel Prize-winning über-genius

Simplicity is the ultimate sophistication.

Leonardo Da Vinci, the original Renaissance Man

Habit is overcome by habit.

Desiderius Erasmus, Dutch Renaissance
humanist and theologian

*The more minutely you describe, the more you will
confuse the mind of the reader and the more you will
prevent him from a knowledge of the thing described...*

Leonardo Da Vinci, the original Renaissance Man

*The important thing in science is not so much to
obtain new facts as to discover new ways of thinking
about them.*

Sir William Henry Bragg: Nobel Prize-winning
scientist and mathematician

*Any intelligent fool can make things bigger and more
complex... It takes a touch of genius—and a lot of courage
to move in the opposite direction.*

Albert Einstein, Nobel Prize-winning über-genius
(attributed)

[What is needed is] a lively intellectual curiosity, an interest in everything – because everything really is connected to everything else, and therefore to what you're trying to do, whatever it is.

From Futurist Harlan Cleveland's *Eight Indispensable Attitudes for Effective Leadership of Complexity*, from his book *Nobody In Charge: Essays on the Future of Leadership*

Medieval Freemasons [also] considered the pentagram to be a symbol of deep wisdom.

Jeremy Harwood, *The Freemasons*

You never change things by fighting the existing reality. To change something, build a new model that makes the existing model obsolete.

R. Buckminster Fuller, Divine Code genius

A work necessary for all the clear-sighted and inquiring human minds, in which everyone who loves to study philosophy, perspective, painting, sculpture, architecture, music and other mathematical disciplines will find a very delicate, subtle and admirable teaching and will delight in diverse questions touching a very secret science.

Fra Luca Pacioli, Da Vinci's mentor and "the Father of Accounting," from his introduction to *The Divine Proportion*

Inspiration, even passion is indeed necessary for creative art, but the knowledge of the Science of Space, of the Theory of Proportions, far from narrowing the creative power of the artist, opens for him an infinite variety of choices within the realm of [symphonic] composition.

Matila Ghyka; Romanian mathematician, aristocrat and author, *The Geometry of Art and Life*

The secrets of the Universe can be divined in a Nautilus shell.

Matthew Cross, inspired by a contemporary Romanian high school mathematics teacher

The principle of information coding by the brain seems to be based on the Golden Mean... [the] insight that the measurement of any physical quantity and quality is based on repetitions of the Golden Mean, opens an astounding variety of possibilities to encode and decode information in the most efficient way. With this property, the brain can use simultaneously the powers of the Golden Mean and the infinite Fibonacci word (synonymously called the golden string, the golden sequence, or the rabbit sequence) for coding and classifying...

Harald Weiss and Volkmar Weiss, *The Golden Mean as Clock Cycle of Brain Waves*, from *Chaos, Solitons and Fractals 18 (2003) No. 4*, 643-652 – Elsevier Author Gateway, online version

The wisest and noblest teacher is Nature itself.

Leonardo Da Vinci, the original Renaissance Man

Some of the greatest mathematical minds of all ages, from Pythagoras and Euclid in ancient Greece, through the medieval Italian mathematician Leonardo of Pisa and the Renaissance astronomer Johannes Kepler, to present-day scientific figures such as Oxford physicist Roger Penrose, have spent endless hours over this simple ratio and its properties. But the fascination with the Golden Ratio is not confined just to mathematicians. Biologists, artists, musicians, historians, architects, psychologists, and even mystics have pondered and debated the basis of its ubiquity and appeal...

Mario Livio, *The Golden Ratio: The Story of Phi, The World's Most Astonishing Number*

The fundamental element in that joy which the artist's creation gives us may well be the manifestation of those profound laws of nature which in some cases, he may have deeply studied, and, in many more he may have so instinctively appreciated that they are the unconscious motives of his style and sense of taste. If Phi [the Golden Ratio] in some way describes the principle of growth, which is one revelation of the spirit of Nature, would not the artist most in touch with Nature tend to employ that proportion in his work, even though he were not conscious of its existence?

Sir Theodore Andrea Cook, *The Curves of Life*

(Use of the Divine Proportion)... seem(s) to be incorporated into many works of art inadvertently, as a product of the artist's aesthetic intuition. However,... in the case of Leonardo, (it was) employed after experimentation and applied with full premeditation.

Bulent Atalay, *Math and The Mona Lisa*

The Golden Ratio is a universal law in which is contained the ground-principle of all formative striving for beauty and completeness in the realms of both nature and art, and which permeates, as a paramount spiritual ideal, all structures, forms and proportions, whether cosmic or individual, organic or inorganic, acoustic or optical; which finds its fullest realization, however, in the human form.

Adolf Zeising, nineteenth century German Golden Ratio researcher & scientist

Understanding and utilizing the Divine Code is best approached with a curious and open mind. Like a Russian Matryoshka nesting doll set, each new level of discovery inevitably leads to another. Be open to the unexpected insights that come from both focused and playful contemplation. The spark of genius does not always ignite according to conscious plan; instead, it often follows a path of revelation uniquely suited to each seeker.

Matthew Cross

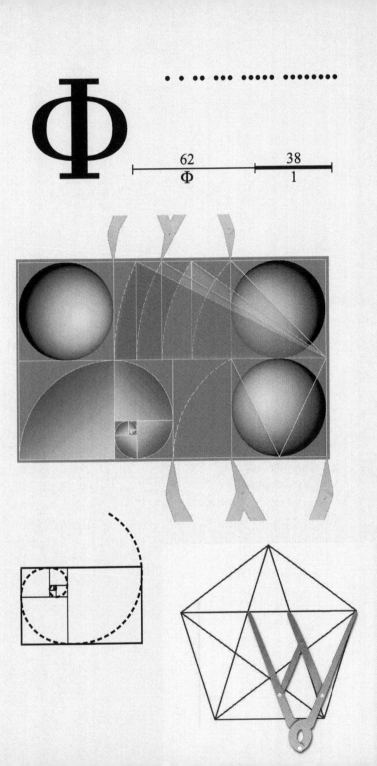

13

Golden Ratio (Phi) & Geometry

The Divine Proportion is a scale of proportions which makes the bad difficult [to produce] and the good easy.

Albert Einstein, Nobel Prize-winning über-genius, in a letter to Divine Code artist and architect Le Corbusier

Nature's Path of Least Resistance and Maximum Performance follows the Golden Mean.

Dr. Ron Sandler, peak performance pioneer

Let no one who is not a mathematician read my works.

Leonardo Da Vinci, the original Renaissance Man

How many pairs of rabbits can be produced from a single pair in one year, if it is assumed that every month each pair begets a new pair, which from the second month becomes productive?

Leonardo Fibonacci, from the third section of *Liber Abaci* [per *Encyclopedia Britannica*], which introduced the Fibonacci numbers and Sequence (the exponentially increasing numbers of rabbit pairs follows the Fibonacci Sequence: 0,1,1,2,5,8, 13,21,34,55,89,144,233,377...)

Numbers really aren't important, it's the ratio that is.

Jeff Wertz, referring to the Golden Ratio in *Wood* Magazine

Plato… [considered the] Golden Section proportion the most binding of all mathematical relations, and makes it the key to the physics of the cosmos.

Peter Tompkins, *Secrets of the Great Pyramid*

The Golden Ratio manifests in the whole of creation. Take the ratio of the length of a man and the height of his navel. The ratio of the sides of the Great Temple. The ratio between the long and short sides of a pentagram. Why is this? Because the ratio of the Whole to the Greater is the ratio of the Greater to the Lesser.

Pythagoras, Greek mathematician

There is geometry in the humming of the strings; there is music in the spacing of the spheres.

Pythagoras, Greek mathematician

If we disregard due proportion by giving anything what is too much for it; too much canvas to a boat, too much nutriment to a body, too much authority to a soul, the consequence is always shipwreck.

Plato, Greek philosopher

Geometry has two great treasures. One is the theorem of Pythagoras, the other, the division of a line into extreme and mean [Golden] ratio. The first we may compare to a measure of gold; the second we may name a precious jewel.

Johannes Kepler, formulator
of the Laws of Planetary Motion

In human endeavor and in all living forms and matter, the closer movement and function is to the Divine Code, the more efficient, beautiful and successful.

Matthew Cross and Robert Friedman, M.D.

Where there is matter, there is geometry.

Johannes Kepler, formulator
of the Laws of Planetary Motion

A straight line is said to have been cut in extreme and mean ratio when, as the whole line is to the greater segment, so is the greater to the lesser.

Euclid, Greek "Father of Geometry"

[The value of Phi is] the key to universal physics.

Sir Edward Victor Appleton, Nobel Prize-winning physicist and radio wave pioneer, whose work proved the existence of the Ionosphere and led to the development of Radar

When we look out on the world, our view of it is framed by the overall limits of our peripheral vision and the centre-line of the eye in its vertical axis is set almost exactly on its 'golden mean'. Moreover, the horizontal axis cuts the maximum eye movement zone, again on its 'golden mean' (if we take the horizontal axis to be the centre-line between the upper and lower limits of our peripheral vision, that is the centre-line of our overall field of view which, coincidentally is the normal declination of the fovea, (area of sharpest visual acuity) when standing 'attentive')...our overall view of the world is still framed by the proportion of a golden rectangle.

Bryan Avery, *Beauty is in the Eye of the Beholder; The Architectural Review*, July 1992

The Golden Number is a product not of mathematical imagination but of a natural principle related to the laws of equilibrium.

Mehmet Suat Bergil, *Doğada/Bilimde/Sanatta, Altyn Oran (The Golden Ratio in Nature/Science/Art)*

The ratios of the line segments in the pentacle [the five-pointed, Golden Star] all equal PHI, making this symbol the ultimate symbol of the Divine Proportion. For this reason, the five-pointed star has always been a symbol of beauty and perfection associated with the Goddess and the sacred feminine.

Dan Brown, *The Da Vinci Code*

The relationship between the ubiquitous logarithmic [Golden] spiral and the Fibonacci number sequence is especially intriguing...

Dr. John Casti, *Complexificaton*

...PHI (1.618) is the Most Beautiful Number in the Universe...

Dan Brown, *The Da Vinci Code*

At its precise Golden Ratio division point—62% of the way through—the #1 video in music history (Michael Jackson's Thriller) reaches its electrifying climax.

Matthew Cross and Robert Friedman, M.D.

You sure find mathematics in the darnedest places!

Donald Duck, in *Disney's Donald Duck in Mathmagic Land*

[The Wave Principle] provides a basis and framework within which to study and quantify social behavior and thus serves as an anchor for the undertaking of true social science. The resulting breakthrough is so profound that it requires a new name for the science it makes possible. I think socionomics is a good term.

Robert R. Prechter, Jr., ElliottWave.com

The impulse of all movement and all form is given by Phi.

Schwaller de Lubicz, *The Temple of Man*

Math-buffs and math-phobes alike can celebrate the (Divine Proportion's) wonder... you will never again look at a pyramid, pinecone, or Picasso in the same light.

Dan Brown, *The Da Vinci Code*

...all things that exist can be distinguished through enumeration. Numbers identify things, and also express orderly relationships among things. The essence of numbers relates to the harmonious existence of all things.

Attributed to Arignote, daughter of Pythagoras
and Theano, First Lady of the Golden Mean;
from Mary Ellen Waithe's *A History of Women
Philosophers: Volume I, 600 BC—500 AD*

That the [whole] unit divided into two parts seems beautiful since, from this point of view, the ratio of the smaller part to the bigger one must be equaled to the ratio of the bigger part to the [whole] unit... Mathematicians call the proportion we are talking about, "division in extreme and mean ratio": or the Goldener Schnitt [Golden Cut or Golden Section].

Adolf Zeising, nineteenth century German
Golden Ratio researcher & scientist, referring
to "The Law of Proportion," a term he coined.

The Fibonacci Sequence numbers [0, 1, 1, 2, 3, 5, 8, 13, 21, 34, 55, 89...] are Nature's numbering system. They appear everywhere in Nature, from the leaf arrangement in plants, to the pattern of the florets of a flower, the bracts of a pinecone, or the scales of a pineapple. The Fibonacci numbers are therefore applicable to the growth of every living thing, including a single cell, a grain of wheat, a hive of bees, and even all of mankind.

Stan Grist, Adventurer and Entrepreneur

The entire notion of a 'surprise party' is...based on the pleasure and gratification many of us feel when confronted with...unexpected appearances. Mathematics, and the Golden Ratio in particular, provide a rich treasure of surprises.

Mario Livio, author, *The Golden Ratio: The Story of Phi, The World's Most Astonishing Number*

Fibonacci's numbers are certainly part of a balance or harmony that feels good and looks good. And it sounds good, too. For instance our music is based on the octave of eight notes. The piano keyboard, representing the octave, shows eight white keys and five black keys. This makes 13—a Fibonacci Sequence [...5, 8, 13...]. Moreover, the musical chord that apparently gives the greatest satisfaction to the human ear, the inner part of which is also in the shape of a [Golden] spiral, is the major 6th, while the note E vibrates at a ratio of .62500 [the Golden Ratio] to the note C.

James Wyckoff, *Pyramid Energy*

Occurrences of the Fibonacci Sequence—like the sequence itself—never seem to end. Science can document their existence, but cannot fully explain them.

William Hoffer, author, *Midnight Express* and *Not Without My Daughter*

Writing in the Daily Telegraph, January 21, 1911, I said that there is a very wonderful number which may be called by the Greek letter Phi [the Golden Ratio], of which nobody has heard much as yet, but of which... a great deal is likely to be heard in the course of time. Among other things, it may explain to architects and sculptors and painters, and everybody interested in their work, the true law which underlies beauty of form. This is a number which never could be expressed exactly, however many figures might be used for the purpose.

William Schooling, from the appendix of Theodore Andrea Cook's *The Curves of Life*

...the tension [in the observed atomic particles] comes from the interaction between spins, causing them to magnetically resonate. For these interactions we found a series (scale) of resonant notes: The first two notes show a perfect relationship with each other. Their frequencies (pitch) are in the ratio of 1.618..., which is the Golden Ratio famous from art and architecture... It reflects a beautiful property of the quantum system - a hidden symmetry...

Dr. Radu Coldea of Oxford University, on the discovery of the Golden Ratio hidden in the nanoscale symmetry of the quantum world in *Science* Magazine; January 8, 2010

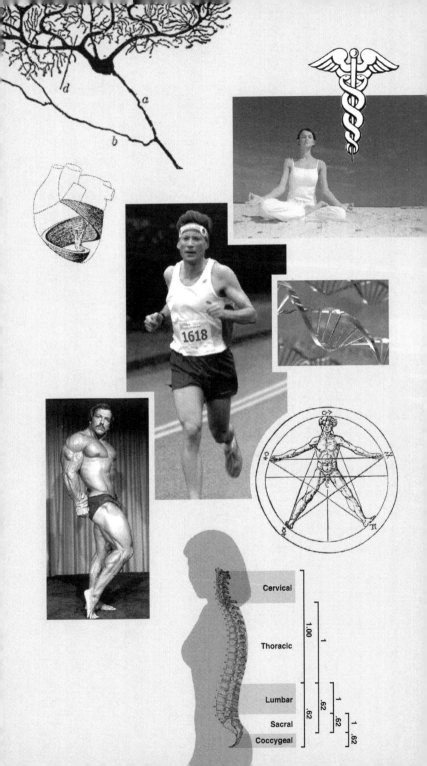

Cervical

Thoracic

Lumbar

Sacral

Coccygeal

1.00

1

.62

.62

1

.62

1

.62

21

Health & Longevity

When Health is absent,
Wisdom cannot reveal itself,
Art cannot become manifest,
Strength cannot be exerted,
Wealth is useless
and Reason is powerless.

Herophilies, 300 B.C., physician
to Alexander the Great

By training in accordance with the Golden Ratio you
virtually eliminate the potential for injury and you can
actually predict with 90% or better accuracy when your
peak day will be, far in advance of your event.

Matthew Cross, on Dr. Ron Sandler's
breakthrough peak performance work

The doctor of the future will give no medicine, but will interest his patients in the care of the human frame, in diet and in the causes and prevention of disease.

Thomas Edison, inventor extraordinaire

Healing is as simple as realigning oneself with the Divine Code.

Robert Friedman, M.D.

The Divine Code is Nature's Universal Thread, with which optimal health is woven.

Robert Friedman, M.D. and Matthew Cross

The unity pattern of cholesterol ratios follows the Divine Code. That is: total cholesterol / LDL = 1.618

Robert Friedman, M.D.

Since the invention of the blood pressure cuff around one hundred years ago, physicians have missed the fascinating observation that blood pressure readings often reflect the Golden Ratio.

Robert Friedman, M.D.

Our bodies have finely-tuned homeostatic mechanisms, which always try to maintain the Golden Ratio with respect to systolic and diastolic blood pressure.

Robert Friedman, M.D.

The single most important biological structure, the DNA molecule, is in PHI (Golden Ratio) proportion.

Stephen Ian McIntosh, Integral theorist and author, *Integral Consciousness and the Future of Evolution*

Eating in Divine Proportion (38% carbohydrates to 62% fat & protein) is ideally a permanent eating pattern.

Robert Friedman, M.D.

By keeping your intake of carbohydrates in Divine Proportion to the amounts of protein and fat eaten, insulin resistance, inflammation and their negative effects can be avoided.

Robert Friedman, M.D.

The magnificence of the structure, function and beauty of the human spine is due to the fact that all of the spinal segments have Divine Code relationships.

Robert Friedman, M.D.

Casey needed only to "tweak" his workouts a little bit more in order to exhibit exact Divine Proportions and actually embody the look of a Greek God.

Robert Friedman, M.D., describing the Divine Code-based Nautilus workouts of bodybuilder Casey Viator

A good stance and posture reflect a proper state of mind.

Morihei Ueishiba, founder of Aikido

About sixty to sixty-five percent [approximating the Golden Ratio] of all the cells in the heart are neural cells which are precisely the same as in the brain, functioning in precisely the same way, monitoring and maintaining control of the entire mind/brain/body physical process as well as direct unmediated connections between the heart and the emotional, cognitive structures of the brain.

Joseph Chilton Pearce,
The Biology of Transcendence

The optimal training ratio is approximately 40% endurance training, 30% strength training and 30% flexibility training. [Golden Ratio of 40% to 60% (30 + 30)]

Dawn Saidur, Olympic sprinter from Bangladesh

Research shows that businessmen who exercise during trips perform 61% [the Golden Ratio] better on tests of alertness and reaction.

Best Life Magazine, June 2006

Your body has a BLUEPRINT [Divine Code], a SCHEMATIC of what perfect health is and it is constantly trying to achieve this perfect health for you. All that goes wrong is that you get in the way of this natural process.

Dr. Richard Schulze, health & longevity pioneer
HerbDoc.com

My advice is if you can nap, do it. If you have a sofa in your office, if you can relax, do it.

Dimitrios Trichopoulos, M.D., lead researcher on a study showing that naps cut heart attacks by 37%

Just as an overloaded washing machine cannot properly wash clothes, an overloaded stomach—over 62% full—cannot properly prepare one's food for optimal digestion.

Matthew Cross

Knowledge and practice of the Golden Ratio is a Golden Key to robust health, happiness and wonder.

Matthew Cross

The Sphere Knot [one of the Spiral Fitness Sticks] is the simplest and most advanced human gear in the history of the planet. It is a Golden Mean proportion of a Fibonacci spiral. It offers a perpetual approach to the martial arts while minimizing blood shed imagery. The shape itself is the perfect contour of sacred geometry and human expression. Spirals of intention flow freely to and fro, expanding and reducing internally and externally without ever crashing into a fracturing halt. This truth holds up at all velocities, allowing the practitioner to resonate at a frequency close to that of plant growth, shaping itself like infinite seashells expressible in all directions.

Rob Moses, Kung Fu master, David Carradine's teacher and creator of the *Spiral Fitness* DVD series KungFuMoses.com

In order to maintain optimal health and weight, our bodies require a Golden Ratio of rest and recovery: between 8 and 9 hours of total sleep/rest every 24 hours.

Matthew Cross & Robert Friedman, M.D.

A full, healthy breath can be broken down into four basic parts—a two-stage inhalation, followed by a two-stage exhalation, with pauses inserted as desired. Practice this breath throughout the day. The breath begins with:

1. A relaxed, full Buddha-belly inhalation, flowing into…

2. A full chest inhalation, while gently pulling in your belly. This supports the rising of your chest, shoulders and head. When you have inhaled just the right amount of air you will feel a sense of satisfaction and relaxation moving through your entire body. You might choose to linger and enjoy for a few moments before cresting the breath wave and…

3. Letting your breath go completely—allowing your lung's natural elasticity to effortlessly contract and exhale—leading into…

4. Pulling your navel into your spine to complete the full exhalation. When your lungs feel "empty," your belly may naturally relax and return to a neutral position, pausing as desired. This naturally flows into…

5. Your next breath… a Golden Breath is when the ratio of inhalation to exhalation approximates 40:60 (the Golden Ratio).

Matthew Cross & Robert Friedman, M.D.

Nobody understood better than Da Vinci the divine structure of the human body… He was the first to show that the human body is literally made of building blocks whose proportions always equal PHI (the Golden Ratio).

Dan Brown, *The Da Vinci Code*

The secret to assuring healthy Divine Code water hydration is simple: don't let your urine get darker than the color of a pale Chardonnay.

Matthew Cross

The more I looked for evidence of the Divine Proportion in the body, the more I was astounded to find it. It was visible in the obvious relationships in the bony skeleton, in the fetal-shaped curves of the organs and in the arborization patterns of the blood vessels, bronchi and nerves. The deeper I looked, the more deeply I discovered this incredible and ubiquitous Code embedded throughout the structure and function of the body, layer upon layer. Even when I moved from the anatomic level to the physiologic level, the fantastic proportionality was still there. From heart rhythms, to blood pressure ratios, to the molecular structure of DNA, the Divine Proportion was abundantly evident. It only followed that the more one could harmonize with this grand principle, the more efficient, effortless and healthy life could be.

Robert Friedman, M.D.

Blood pressure values in "well" individuals, but not in those who are at risk of dying, exhibit the Golden Ratio [i.e., their systolic:diastolic blood pressure was consistently in the 1.618 Golden Ratio range, e.g., 120/75 =1.6 ratio].

Hanno Ulmer, Ph.D, Austrian statistician and medical researcher

34

Love & Relationships

The lover is drawn by the thing loved, as the sense is by that which it perceives...

Leonardo Da Vinci, the original Renaissance Man

It turns out that chocolate, the "Food of the Gods," is also the food of love—and the Divine Code. Chocolate's fat content falls neatly into Golden Ratio distribution, with approximately 62% of its fat being saturated and the remaining 38% being polyunsaturated and monounsaturated. Chocolate also contains small amounts of Phenethylamine, otherwise known as the "love chemical."

Robert Friedman, M.D. and Matthew Cross

Yogi Bhajan used to say that the sperm that makes it in circles the egg 8 times before being accepted. Likewise, a man must often "circle" a woman 8 times before being accepted…

GM Khalsa, Yogi Master, BreathIsLife.com

60% of our communication power is in our body language, e.g., eye contact, facial expression, posture; 30% is in our voice tone, and the remaining 10% is in the actual words we use. This 60/40 (30+10) ratio closely approximates the 62/38 Golden Ratio. Since the top two categories equal 90% of our communication power (body language = 60%, voice tone = 30%) this ought to inspire us to prioritize enhancement efforts especially on our non-verbal and voice tone communication skills.

Matthew Cross

Let there be spaces in your togetherness, and let the winds of the heavens dance between you… Love one another but make not a bond of love: Let it rather be a moving sea between your shores… Sing and dance together and be joyous, but let each one of you be alone, even as the strings of a lute are alone though they quiver with the same music… And stand together, yet not too near together: For the pillars of the temple stand apart, and the oak tree and the cypress grow not in each other's shadow.

Kahlil Gibran, *The Prophet*

A survey of two thousand women in 2003 revealed that, given a choice between cuddling and making love, 62% [the Golden Ratio] preferred to cuddle, while 38% preferred to more immediately make love.

Esquire Magazine, 2003

Early scientific research by Masters & Johnson and others into the physiology of the sexual response identified five stages of lovemaking: 1) foreplay, 2) sexual stimulation, 3) dilatation and erection, 4) orgasm, 5) resolution. When the Golden Ratio is superimposed over these five stages of lovemaking, we find that the onset of orgasm occurs at a point approximately 62% of the way through lovemaking. This means that in order for enjoyable lovemaking and mutually fulfilling orgasms to occur, both partners must honor the early stages of lovemaking—especially foreplay.

Matthew Cross and Robert Friedman, M.D.

When all is said and done, 62% [the Golden Ratio] of woman want a man who makes them laugh, rather than one who can bench his body weight.

McMasters University research, as reported by Lori Buckley, Psy.D. in *Best Life* Magazine, March 2007

55

Nature

[The Golden Mean] is a reminder of the relatedness of the created world to the perfection of its source and of its potential future evolution.

Robert Lawlor, sacred geometer and author, *Sacred Geometry: Philosophy and Practice*

Spirals that approach the mathematical precision of the Golden Spiral can usually be found where the energy of conflicting forces is resolved.

Stephen Ian McIntosh, Integral theorist and author, *Integral Consciousness and the Future of Evolution*

The Golden Section is the Pattern of Life.

John Michell, *The New View Over Atlantis*

The Golden Ratio is Nature's pervasive constant of design.

Gary Meisner, founder of PhiPointSolutions.com

Climb the mountains and get their good tidings; Nature's peace will flow into you as sunshine into flowers, the winds will blow their freshness into you and the storms their energy, and cares will drop off like autumn leaves.

John Muir, renowned naturalist

I wish more life to creative rhythms of great Nature, Nature with a capital N as we spell God with a capital G. Why? Because Nature is all the body of God we mortals will ever see.

Frank Lloyd Wright, legendary architect

I flame above the beauty of the fields; I shine in the waters; In the sun, the moon and the stars, I burn.

Hildegarde von Bingen, Christian mystic
and polymath

A thing may endure in Nature, if it is duly proportioned to its necessity.

Fra Luca Pacioli, Da Vinci's mentor
and the "Father of Accounting"

A Monarch In Flight.
The Summer Flowers Delight.
PHI Found In Nature.

> Hotel Indigo's Fibonacci Haiku, on room cardkey
> jacket, HotelIndigo.com

Paul Green, at Stanford, has argued persuasively that
the Fibonacci series is just what one would expect as
the simplest self-repeating pattern that can be generated
by the particular growth processes in the growing tips
of the tissues that form sunflowers, pinecones, and
so forth. Like a snowflake and its sixfold symmetry,
the pinecone and its phyllotaxis may be part of order
for free.

> Dr. Stuart Kauffman, scientist and
> author of *At Home In The Universe*

It should come as no surprise to discover the two giants
of our solar system reinforcing the Divine Proportion of
life on Earth... The Divine Proportion, long associated
with life—and conspicuously absent from modern
equations—plays lovingly around the Earth. Does this in
some way have something to do with why we are here,
and what we might be?

> Richard Heath in *The Matrix of Creation*, revealing
> that the Divine Proportion defines the relative
> speeds of the orbits of Earth, Jupiter and Saturn in
> space and time to an accuracy of 99.99%

The fact that plants express their leaf arrangement in terms of Fibonacci numbers, so frequently that it passes for the normal case, is proof that [plants] are aiming at the utilization of the Fibonacci angle [in leaf placement], which will give minimum superposition [overlap] and maximum sun and rain assimilation potential for all leaves.

Sir Theodore Andrea Cook, *The Curves of Life*

The Golden Section is the prime geometric and genetic secret of the chambered Nautilus and of many sensitively balanced spiral shells and horns, and it's the key to this self-congruence that enables them to grow year after year without appreciably shifting their centers of gravity.

Guy Murchie, *The Seven Mysteries of Life*

The emotion roused in us by the irresistible beauty of a shell or a flower is due both to the unconscious but continuously instinctive efforts made by the growing organism to adapt itself to its environment, and to the fact that those efforts have been sufficiently successful to express that organisms fitness to survive. Had they been insufficient it would have died. The process of growth explained by the Golden Spiral, and the successive proportions they reveal, have therefore an intimate connection with the source of our pleasure in the beauty of the natural object.

Sir Theodore Andrea Cook, *The Curves of Life*

The Golden Ratio provides flower petals and leaves with maximum exposure to sunlight and allows raindrops to flow down to the roots in the most effective manner. The sunflower positions its seeds in a Golden Ratio Spiral because it is the most effective manner of having as many seeds in a given amount of space possible, allowing them to remain un-crowded within that space...

Edwin Leong, photographer
CameraHobby.com

89

Unity & Spirituality

In the beginning there was the Ratio, and the Ratio was with God, and the Ratio was God.

John 1:1, *The Bible*

Avoid extremes—Keep the Golden Mean.

Cleobus of Lindus, one of the
Seven Wise Men of ancient Greece

The spiral is an archetype embedded deeply in our collective unconscious.

Carl Jung, founder of analytical psychology

Without looking out the window, one may see the way of heaven.

Lao-Tzu, Taoist master

I believe the geometric (Divine) proportion served the Creator as an idea when he introduced the continuous generation of similar objects from similar objects.

Johannes Kepler, formulator of the Laws of Planetary Motion

Since the beginning of time, the Tao has always existed. It is beyond existing and not existing. How do I know where creation comes from? I look inside myself and see it.

Lao-Tzu, Taoist master

Like God, the Divine Proportion is always similar to itself.

Fra Luca Pacioli, Da Vinci's mentor
and the "Father of Accounting"

We're at the birth of an enormously exciting new era. Instead of being citizens of a country, we'll just be Earthlings, with citizen-of-the-world passports.

Sir Richard Branson, Virgin Group Limited founder, entrepreneur, humanitarian

...Perhaps there is a pattern set up in the heavens for one who desires to see it, and having seen it, to find it in himself.

Plato, Greek philosopher

Look beyond the chaos of existence and you see order. It is not utopian or fascistical or like any kind of man-made order, but divine and perfect, and it existed before time. Socrates called it the 'heavenly pattern' which anyone can discover, and once they have found it they can establish it in themselves.

John Michell, author and Divine Code genius,
from his *Confessions of a Radical Traditionalist*

God geometrizes.

Plato, Greek philosopher

(The Golden Ratio is) The Secret of the Universe.

Pythagoras, Greek mathematician

Everyone sees the unseen in proportion to the clarity of his heart, and that depends upon how much he has polished it. Whoever has polished it more sees more— more unseen forms become manifest to him.

Rumi, 13th-century Persian poet

I believe in God, only I spell it 'Nature.'

Frank Lloyd Wright, legendary architect

The Shamans know that energy moves in figure eights, in spirals, through our bodies...

Brant Secunda, Huichol Indian Shaman, teacher and healer

There is nothing pleasurable except that which is in harmony with the utmost depths of our Divine Nature.

Heinrich Suso, German Mystic

When one sees eternity in things that pass away, then one has pure knowledge.

Bhagavad Gita, sacred Hindu scripture

Form and function should be one, joined in a spiritual union.

Frank Lloyd Wright, legendary architect

Every part is disposed to unite with the whole, that it may thereby escape from its own incompleteness.

Leonardo Da Vinci, the original Renaissance Man

The pharaonic Egyptians, says Schwaller de Lubicz [French philosopher, archeologist and author] considered Phi not as a number, but as a symbol of the creative function, or of reproduction in an endless series: to them it represented 'the fire of life, the male action of sperm, the logos of the gospel of St. John.'

Peter Tompkins, *Secrets of the Great Pyramid*

In response to the question "Are you a fan of the Fibonacci Sequence?" U2's Bono replied: "How can you not be? It's everywhere; it's all around."

Michael Castine, former White House official

...The Fibonacci Series... shows up all over the place in Nature; nobody knows exactly why...

MIT Professor Noam Chomsky,
world-renowned linguist, political analyst
and author, *Manufacturing Consent*

Proportion is not only to be found in numbers and measures, but also in sounds, weights, intervals of time, and in every active force in existence.

Leonardo Da Vinci, the original Renaissance Man

The Fibonacci Sequence is a metaphor of the human quest for order and harmony among chaos.

Mario Merz, modern Italian Divine Code artist

Nature is the realization of the simplest conceivable mathematical ideas. ...I am convinced that we can discover by means of purely mathematical constructions the concepts and the laws connecting them with each other.

Albert Einstein, Nobel Prize-winning über-genius
Oxford lecture, 1933

The golden relationship is an expression of unity—a unity pattern—because each part is defined completely by its relation to the whole.

Stephen Ian McIntosh, Integral theorist and author,
Integral Consciousness and the Future of Evolution

It is impossible to join two things in a beautiful manner without a third being present, for a bond must exist to unite them, and this bond is best achieved by a proportion.

Plato, Greek philosopher

[According to Plato, the Golden Ratio-based Dodecahedron is the solid] which God used for embroidering the constellations on the whole of heaven.

David Darling, *The Universal Book of Mathematics*

The Divine Proportion [Golden Ratio] is the sacred code by which the religions of the world have fractalized the sense of God or oneness into the duality of our world... The Divine Proportion can thus be understood as a graphic description of 'the three that are two that are one.' This expression of the first division of unity is symbolic of the original act that created the universe of time and space... Jesus of Nazareth said: 'He who has seen me has seen the Father.'

This [above] statement shows how Jesus can be understood as a representation of the Golden Mean. That is, in the Christian tradition of the human Jesus—the Son of Man (the small part)—is to the divine Jesus—the Son of God (the large part)— as Jesus the Son of God is to God the Father (the whole)... A fundamental teaching of many of the world's great spiritual traditions is that God lives in each and every one of us—that the Creator is the seed of the created. And this is the primary theological message of the self-similar unity of the Golden Mean.

Stephen Ian McIntosh, Integral theorist and author, *Integral Consciousness and the Future of Evolution*

When we have unified enough certain knowledge, we will understand who we are and why we are here.

Edward O. Wilson, Harvard professor and scientist, *Consilience: The Unity of Knowledge*

Just like God cannot be properly defined, nor can be understood through words, likewise our [Divine] proportion cannot be ever designated by intelligible numbers, nor can it be expressed by any rational quantity, but always remains concealed and secret, and is called irrational by the mathematicians.

Fra Luca Pacioli, Da Vinci's mentor
and the "Father of Accounting"

The chaos of the world has an underlying order. When the ancients discovered Phi, they were certain they had stumbled across God's building block for the world, and they worshipped Nature because of that.

Dan Brown, *The Da Vinci Code*

The Fibonacci Sequence turns out to be the key to understanding how nature designs... and is... a part of the same ubiquitous music of the spheres that builds harmony into atoms, molecules, crystals, shells, suns and galaxies and makes the universe sing.

Guy Murchie, *The Seven Mysteries of Life*

To be practical about it, how have I used Phi in my life? I really used the Golden Mean as a master motif of everything in my company [Now-Zen.com] that we've done, not just in the design of the products and marketing materials, but even in the distribution of stock. It's a ratio, it's more of a relationship, so any time there's an opportunity to form a relationship, I think about [it and ask myself] 'OK, what seems fair, what's right or does that look good?' I'll do it without thinking about the Golden Mean. Then I'll bring the Golden Mean in as a check. And if it's close I'll adjust it to the Golden Mean. So, I'm not a slave to it [the Mean], but I always use it as a way of aligning what my intuition is telling me how to set up the best relationship for beauty or any kind of quality like that. I guess the best thing I can say about the Golden Mean is that it's helped me to understand unity, what the real meaning of unity is.

Stephen Ian McIntosh, Integral theorist and author, *Integral Consciousness and the Future of Evolution*

Man is the measure of all things.

Protagoras, pre-Socratic Greek philosopher

Know Thyself... In True Proportion.

What some suggest was written
above the Oracle at Delphi

We come spinning out of nothingness,
scattering stars like dust.

Rumi, 13th-century Persian poet

This book was designed to be a catalyst for your awakening to the Divine Code.

If you would like to learn more about the Secret Code of the Universe and it's practical applications to everyday life, read our definitive works on the subject, ***The Divine Code of Da Vinci, Fibonacci, Einstein and YOU*** and ***The Divine Code Lifestyle Diet.***

Available at:
TheDivineCode.com

Create Your Own Customized Fibonacci Sequence

Leonardo Fibonacci's "rabbit riddle" first delineated the infinite and mysterious Sequence that bears his name—where each successive number is always the sum of the previous two: 0, 1, 1, 2, 3, 5, 8, 13, 21... This Sequence gives rise to the Golden Ratio: 1.618... that elusive, infinite number approached ever more closely by the ratio of any two successive numbers in the Sequence. Yet, the Golden Ratio is not specific to Fibonacci's Sequence.

Did you know that you can derive your own customized Sequence that will generate Golden Ratio approximations? Any two numbers added together will generate a third number, which when added to the previous number will give rise to another. When repeated around 6 to 10 times, this additive process will begin to generate successive numbers that form ever-finer Golden Ratio approximations. Fibonacci's genius was describing the base fractal of this process starting with 0, 1, 1... You can create your own customized version using any two numbers that have meaning for you. A common method is to use the first two numbers of your birthday, a method was described by Bulent Atalay in his excellent book, *Math and the Mona Lisa: The Art and Science of Leonardo da Vinci.*

Try it: Take your birth month and date and add them together to get a third number. For example, June 18th would be 6/18. Adding them together gives 24.

Then, combine this third number with the one before it to produce a fourth number. Repeat this process and you'll find that after 6 to 10 times, the ratio between your unique numbers always converges to 1.618... The Golden Ratio!

$$6 + 18 = 24 \quad 24 + 18 = 42 \quad 42 + 24 = 66$$
$$66 + 42 = 108 \quad 108 + 66 = 174 \quad 174 + 108 = 282$$
$$282 + 174 = 456 \quad 456 + 282 = 738$$

Then, divide the last two sequential numbers: $738 \div 456 = 1.618...$ The actual Sequence in this example would be: 6, 18, 24, 42, 66, 108, 174, 282, 456, 738... In this case, the Golden Ratio 1.618 showed up after the 8th iteration. You can check the ratios at each stage to see how close you're getting to 1.618. If you have a Fibonacci birthday (1/1, 1/2, 2/3, 3/5, 5/8 or 8/13) then you know where this is going fast!

Now, your turn. Fill in your two selected start numbers in the shaded areas at number one below to begin your customized Fibonacci Sequence. Check your ratios as you go, to see how many iterations you need before you reach the Golden Ratio (accurate to four digits) of 1.618...

(1) _____ + _____ = _____
                                       ratio

(2) _____ + _____ = _____
                                       ratio

(3) _____ + _____ = _____
                                       ratio

(4) _____ + _____ = _____
                                       ratio

(5) _____ + _____ = _____
                                       ratio

(6) _____ + _____ = _____
                                       ratio

(7) _____ + _____ = _____
                                       ratio

(8) _____ + _____ = _____
                                       ratio

(9) _____ + _____ = _____
                                       ratio

(10) _____ + _____ = _____
                                       ratio

(11) _____ + _____ = _____
                                       ratio

13 Divine Code
Book Recommendations

***The Divine Code of Da Vinci, Fibonacci,
Einstein & YOU***
Matthew Cross & Robert Friedman, M.D.;
Hoshin Media Group: 2009

The Divine Code Lifestyle Diet
Robert Friedman, M.D. & Matthew Cross;
Hoshin Media Group: 2010

The Da Vinci Code
Dan Brown; particularly Chapter 20 (on PHI)

The Golden Section: Nature's Greatest Secret
Scott Olsen

***A Beginner's Guide to Constructing the
Universe: Mathematical Archetypes of Nature,
Art and Science***
Michael Schneider; particularly Chapter 5

The Elliott Wave Principle
Robert Prechter, Jr.

***The Power of Limits: Proportional Harmonies
in Nature, Art, and Architecture***
Gyorgy Doczi

***Fabulous Fibonacci's: Mystery
and Magic in Numbers***
Trudi Hammel Garland

***The Golden Ratio: The Story of PHI,
the World's Most Astonishing Number,***
Mario Livio

***Divine Proportion: Phi in Art,
Nature, and Science***
Priya Hemenway

***Leonard of Pisa and the Mathematics
of the Middle Ages***
Joseph and Frances Gies

Secrets of the Great Pyramid
Peter Tompkins; particularly chapter XV,
The Golden Section

Fibonacci's Liber Abaci
[translated] Laurence Sigler

Web Sites

www.TheDivineCode.com
Home site for the Divine Code book series; loaded with books, DVDs, resources, news and links.

www.HoshinMedia.com
Publisher of The Divine Code series and Matthew Cross' books and media.

www.MillionairesMap.com
Matthew Cross' book site; includes a sample chapter.

www.LeadershipAlliance.com
Matthew Cross' business organization site. Breakthrough strategies for growth and transformation.

www.CineVisionProductions.com
Robert Friedman, M.D.'s site for cutting edge movements and exercises.

www.CineVisionProductions.com
Robert Friedman, M.D.'s DVD programs.

www.618Design.com
Home site for the Divine Code master designer Tom Reczek.

www.Abraham-Hicks.com
Home site for the life transforming teachings of Abraham.

www.BeautyAnalysis.com
Site to see the Golden Ratio based beauty
mask and other Golden Ratio information.

www.ElliottWave.com
Robert Prechter, Jr.'s Elliott Wave International site.

www.CafePress.com/georgegreer
George Greer's colorful Golden Rectangle organic
cotton T-Shirt designs.

www.JoelBarker.com
Paradigm pioneer Joel Barker's site.

www.ManagementWisdom.com
Quality genius Dr. W. Edwards Deming treasury:
The Deming Video Library, Books, Articles, Resources.

www.PhiPointSolutions.com
Great resource for all things Phi/Golden Ratio;
Gary Meisner's home site.

www.BreathIsLife.com
Home site of Yoga Master Gurumarka.

www.Arihanto.com
Home site of artist/healer Ari Hanto, who offers
transformational energetic artwork, personal and
remote healing sessions. She uniquely blends person-
alized flower essences into her watercolors, which
give her paintings their characteristic healing energy.

http://milan.milanovic.org/math/index.php
Rasko Jovanovic's World of Mathematics. Fantastic
Fibonacci and Golden Section resource.

About the Authors

Matthew Cross is President of Leadership Alliance, a cutting-edge consulting firm providing breakthrough strategies for growth and transformation. A Deming Quality Scholar, author, international speaker and Hoshin Kanri strategic alignment master, he is in high demand for his ability to help people and organizations navigate to their highest success. He works with individuals and Fortune 100 companies around the world. He is also a principle in Total Performance Training, a consortium dedicated to supporting people, teams and companies to discover their genius, live their potential and make a difference. Matthew is also an ancient history researcher and competitive athlete (running and tennis). Matthew can be reached at: MCross@LeadersAll.com

Robert Friedman, M.D. practiced nutritional and preventive medicine in Santa Fe, New Mexico for 25 years before turning his attention to sacred geometry and its application to health and longevity. Dr. Friedman is also the originator of the Spiral~Chi Evolutionary Movement system based on spinal and spiral wave motions, which has been compared to a synthesis of yoga and tai chi and emphasizes tuning in to one's own natural spiral nature. Dr. Friedman can be reached at: DrBob@TheDivineCode.com.

A-Z Quote Author's Index

Picture Credits

A heartfelt THANK YOU to every person and organization who graciously allowed us to include their excellent pictures in our book. The authors would also like to extend a special thanks to Jimmy Wales, founder of Wikipedia.org, which facilitated easy and enjoyable access to many of the great public domain pictures featured in the book. Please know that every effort has been made to assure that all credits are accurately attributed. If any omission or discrepancy is discovered, please notify the publisher. *Thank you.*

Wineglass (modified by the authors), Nautilus shells, Sunflower, Hummingbird (modified by the authors), Starfish, Ocean Wave, Ram, Sand dollar, Great Pyramid, Mandelbrot fractal, Head X-Ray (Golden Spiral added by authors), Michelangelo's David, DNA chrome model, Loving swans, Buddha, Ankh, Cross, Yoga woman, Cash stack: iStockPhoto.com • Man/Gears (woodcut): Camille Flammarion, 1888, from his L'atmosphère: météorologie populaire, Flag, Galaxy, Parthenon, Leonardo Da Vinci self-portrait, Fra Luca Pacioli, Albert Einstein, *Mona Lisa* (Golden Ratio study work added by the authors), Human spine (modified by the authors), E=mc^2/Germany, 1 Euro coin, Marilyn Monroe, Brain dendrites, Pentagram man, Da Vinci's The Last Supper, Michelangelo's Oracle of Delphi, Phi symbol, Caduceus, Abduction of Psyche and Dawn by Bouguereau, Authors-modified fresco by Giorgio Vasari (Duomo Santa Maria Del Fiore, Florence, Italy) photo by Thermos: Wikipedia.org • Fibonacci statue, DNA w/ Golden Ratios, Elliott Wave graph: Robert R. Prechter, Jr. / The Elliott Wave Principle. • Credit Card: Nikylla Celine. • Notre Dame/calipers, Pentagram w/ Phi growth, Broccoli, Golden Rectangle w/ Golden Spiral, Bee w/ calipers, Golden Ratio "Divine Pulse" graph: Steven Ian McIntosh / The Golden Mean Book. • iPod®, iPhone®: Apple Inc. • Portrait of JFK Copyright ©1967 by Jamie Wyeth; Golden Ratio grid added by the authors: Courtesy of Jamie Wyeth / www.JamieWyeth.com • Heart spiral muscle: J. Bell Pettigrew / The Bakken, Minneapolis, MN. • Fibonacci rabbit graph, Pentagram drawing, Cornucopia w/ cash, Rose, Divine code glyph(s), Golden Ratio grid, Lightbulb, Brain Waves, MindMap, Angel statue, Double spiral tree trunk, Runner, Vitruvian Man w/ DNA Spiral, Hand w/ Golden Spiral, Old coin: Matthew Cross. • Pinecone, Golden Ratio Orgasm graph: Robert Friedman, M.D. • 62/38 Golden Ratio pie graph, Pentagram w/ ratios: Robert Friedman, M.D. Matthew Cross and Tom Reczek. • Julia Set Crop Circle: Colin Andrews, www.ColinAndrews.net • Author Matthew Cross: Author's collection • Author Robert Friedman, M.D.: Kim Jew, KimJewPhotography.com • Pentagram w/ calipers: Dr. Eddie Levin / www.goldenmeangauge.co.uk • (Root five plus one) over two—Golden Ratio generation art (caliper tips added by the authors): Courtesy of Scott Onstott, ScottOnstott.com. • Double wave collision: Andrew Castellano, www.Flickr.com/photo/acastellano. • Casey Viator: Courtesy of Casey Viator. • Commissioned Divine Code Woman by Chloe Hedden, www.ChloeHedden.com; © 2010 Matthew Cross.

Notes

Notes

From Hoshin Media

Hoshin Success Compass™

Map Your Way to Success with the
Secret Alignment Process of the World's
Greatest Companies, such as Proctor &
Gamble, Toyota and Bank of America.

by Matthew Cross

*Hoshin Media, 2010;
illustrated workbook. • $19.95*

The Millionaire's MAP™

Chart Your Way to Wealth
& Abundance by Tapping the
Infinite Power of Your Imagination.

by Matthew Cross

*Hoshin Media, 2010;
illustrated workbook. • $24.95*

62 Smashing Success Secrets, Tools & Strategies

Simple, Profound Keys for Activating & Living
Your Full Passion & Potential in Life and Business.

by Matthew Cross

Hoshin Media, 2011; illustrated. • $14.95

Be Your Own President

An Interactive Handbook for Personal & Professional
Leadership & Transformation.

by Matthew Cross

Hoshin Media, 2011; illustrated workbook. • $19.95

The Little Book
of Romanian Wisdom

Discover the heart, soul and
unique wisdom of Romania.

by Diana Doroftei & Matthew Cross

Hoshin Media, 2010; illustrated. • *$12.95*

Evolutionary Movement DVD from
Robert Friedman, M.D.

Spiral~Chi

Learn How to Combine
Spinal Waves and Spirals for
the Ultimate in Stretching
and Strengthening.
The Next Evolution
in Movement Therapy.

Robert Friedman, M.D.

DVD 43 min. $29.95 order at
www.CineVisionProductions.com

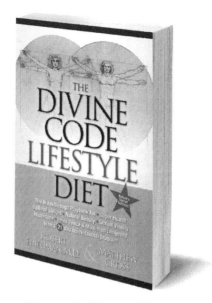

Discover Nature's Secret Nutrient
for Vibrant Health & Longevity

The Divine Code Lifestyle Diet ventures boldly into new territory in the fields of health, nutrition and longevity—where no doctor, nutritionist or personal trainer has gone before. This revolutionary approach to high-level wellness takes a Copernican jump into the Golden Ratio fundamentals of physiology, nutrition and human potential. You are guided into an easily understandable, yet expanded view of how Nature's Universal Design Code is at the core of restoring your optimal health and vitality. You will learn how to access Nature's Secret Nutrient and partake of its essence immediately by using *The Divine Code Lifestyle Diet's* 21-Day Quick Start program. This unique Diet is guaranteed to be unlike any other you've ever tried or heard of. Packed with fascinating and practical insights, tips and techniques, it's a truly revolutionary way to upgrade every aspect of your life.

by Robert Friedman, M.D. & Matthew Cross

Hoshin Media, 2010; 425 pages; illustrated. • $19.95

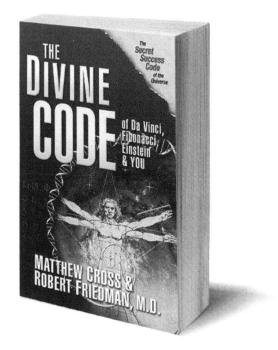

A Tour de Force into the Secret Success Code of the Universe

A treasure chest encyclopedia on the history, pioneering geniuses and practical applications of PHI/the Golden Ratio 1.618:1, the Secret Success Code of the Universe.

In the Divine Code, Matthew Cross and Dr. Robert Friedman take one of Creation's greatest secrets and make it accessible, engaging and fun.

Michael J. Gelb, best-selling author of
How To Think Like Leonardo Da Vinci

By Matthew Cross & Robert Friedmna, M.D.

Hoshin Media, 2009; 660 pages; illustrated. • *$29.95*

Made in the USA
Charleston, SC
01 October 2010